UNSEEN WOUNDS

Understanding and Addressing Elder Abuse.

By
Danish Ali Bajwa & Usama Bajwa

Copyright © 2023 By RK Books Publication

The content contained within this book may not be reproduced, duplicated, or transmitted in any form or retrieval system now known or to be invented without direct written permission from the author or publisher. Under no circumstances will any blame or legal responsibility be held against the publisher, or author, for any damages, reparation, or monetary loss due to the information contained within this book. Either directly or indirectly.

Legal Notice:

This book is copyright protected. This book is only for personal use. You cannot amend, distribute, sell, use, quote, or paraphrase any part of the content within this book without the author or publisher's consent. "Fair Use" means a summary or quote with appropriate credit to the author is permitted.

Disclaimer Notice:

Please note the information contained within this book is for educational purposes only. All effort has been executed to present accurate, up-to-date, reliable, and complete information. No warranties of any kind are declared or implied. Readers acknowledge that the author is not rendering legal, financial, medical, or professional advice. The content within this book has been derived from various sources. Please consult a qualified professional before attempting any techniques outlined in this book. By reading and using this book, the reader agrees that under no circumstances is the author responsible for any direct or indirect losses incurred due to the use of the information within this book, including, but not limited to, — errors, omissions, or inaccuracies.

Email: rkbooks16@gmail.com

EBOOK ISBN: 978-969-3492-12-5

PAPERBACK ISBN: 978-969-3492-13-2

HARDBACK ISBN: 978-969-3492-14-9

Authors Bio

Danish Ali Bajwa and Usama Bajwa, collectively known as the Bajwa Brothers, are a dynamic writing duo known for their vast array of published works spanning several genres. Born and raised in a home where creativity and knowledge were deeply valued, these brothers harnessed their intrinsic knack for storytelling and exploration into a thriving career in literature.

Danish Ali Bajwa is a prolific writer with a unique ability to connect with a diverse audience. With a distinct voice, he has contributed to an extensive collection of children's books, where he elegantly interweaves essential life lessons with engaging narratives that resonate with young minds. Beyond children's literature, Usama's portfolio also includes a number of motivational books. He has an uncanny knack for uplifting and inspiring readers through his compelling narratives and authentic portrayals of the human spirit. Usama's words serve as a beacon of positivity, inspiring readers to conquer their fears and reach their true potential.

Usama Bajwa, on the other hand, brings an analytical perspective to their writing collaboration. With a keen interest in the intersection of business and technology, Danish has written several informative books, making complex topics accessible and engaging for readers. Danish's expertise in business and tech-related subjects is evident in his comprehensive and intuitive guides. He excels at presenting innovative ideas and futuristic trends with a grounded understanding of contemporary business needs, making his books a staple in the libraries of ambitious entrepreneurs and tech enthusiasts.

Together, Danish and Usama have cultivated a unique and diverse writing style that captivates their readers, keeping them engrossed from the first page to the last. Their books often reflect the symbiosis of their different interests and expertise, and the powerful balance between emotion and logic. Despite their varied interests, they share a commitment to creating high-quality literature that is both engaging and enlightening. The Bajwa Brothers continue to establish their presence in the literary world, building a legacy of insightful, thought-provoking, and enchanting books that truly make a difference.

Preface

Welcome to "Unseen Wounds: Understanding and Addressing Elder Abuse." This book aims to shine a light on a pervasive and often overlooked issue that affects the lives of older adults worldwide—elder abuse. It is a comprehensive resource that explores the various dimensions of elder abuse, provides valuable insights into its impact, and offers strategies to address and prevent this form of mistreatment.

Elder abuse is a deeply concerning and distressing problem that is prevalent in both developed and developing countries. However, it remains largely hidden behind closed doors, leaving the wounds inflicted upon older adults unseen by society. These wounds can be physical, emotional, financial, or the result of neglect, and they have a profound impact on the well-being and quality of life of older adults.

The motivation behind this book is to raise awareness, promote understanding, and inspire action to combat elder abuse. By delving into the intricacies of this issue, we hope to empower readers to recognize the signs of elder abuse, respond effectively, and contribute to the prevention of mistreatment in their communities and beyond.

In the following chapters, we will embark on a journey of exploration and education. We will begin by defining elder abuse and providing an overview of its different forms, including physical, emotional, financial, and neglect. Each chapter will delve into these forms in detail, exploring their characteristics, manifestations, and the impact they have on older adults.

Understanding the root causes and contributing factors of elder abuse is essential to developing effective strategies for prevention and intervention. In subsequent chapters, we will examine the social, cultural, and economic determinants that underpin elder abuse. By exploring these factors, we aim to foster a deeper understanding of the complexities surrounding elder abuse and identify pathways for change.

Recognizing that prevention is key to combating elder abuse, we will explore strategies for creating age-friendly environments, promoting awareness, and fostering a culture of respect for older adults. We believe that by cultivating a society that values and cherishes its elders, we can establish a strong foundation for the prevention of elder abuse.

Throughout this book, we will emphasize the importance of support and healing for elder abuse survivors. We will delve into the long-term consequences of abuse and the impact it has on the physical and emotional well-being of older adults. By exploring trauma-informed care, counseling, and support services, we aim to provide guidance and resources for those working with survivors of elder abuse.

This book also takes a global perspective on elder abuse. Recognizing that this issue transcends geographical, cultural, and socioeconomic boundaries, we will explore cross-cultural perspectives and examine the challenges faced by different societies in addressing elder abuse. By understanding the cultural contexts in which abuse occurs, we can develop culturally sensitive strategies that resonate with diverse communities.

It is our hope that this book will serve as a catalyst for change—a call to action for individuals, communities, organizations, and policymakers to prioritize the well-being and rights of older adults. We believe that by shining a light on elder abuse, fostering awareness, and equipping readers with knowledge and tools, we can collectively work towards a future where elder abuse is eradicated, and older adults are protected, respected, and valued.

We invite you to embark on this journey with us—to explore the depths of elder abuse, to understand its impact, and to be inspired to take action. By doing so, we can create a world where older adults can age with dignity, security, and the support they deserve. Together, let us bring the unseen wounds of elder abuse into the light and work towards a society that cherishes and protects its elder population.

Contents

Introduction 1

Chapter 1 Defining Elder Abuse 4

    Types of Elder Abuse 4

    Recognizing the Signs of Elder Abuse 7

Chapter 2 Understanding the Impact of Elder Abuse 10

    Physical, Emotional, and Psychological Effects of Elder Abuse 13

    Complex Interplay of Physical, Emotional, and Psychological Effects 14

    Long-Term Consequences on Health and Well-being 16

Chapter 3 Exploring the Factors Contributing to Elder Abuse 20

    Social Isolation and Loneliness in Relation to Elder Abuse 23

    Caregiver Stress and Burnout in Relation to Elder Abuse 26

    Financial Strain and Exploitation in Relation to Elder Abuse 30

Chapter 4 Identifying Vulnerable Populations in Relation to Elder Abuse 35

    Dementia and Cognitive Impairment in Relation to Elder Abuse .. 39

    Vulnerabilities to Elder Abuse 40

    Elderly Individuals with Disabilities in Relation to Elder Abuse ... 44

Minority and Underserved Communities in Relation to Elder Abuse 47

Chapter 5 Reporting Elder Abuse: Legal and Ethical Considerations 52

Ethical Responsibilities of Professionals and Individuals 53

Approaches to Intervention and Support in Elder Abuse 56

Intervention Strategies:Safety Planning 57

Chapter 6 Preventing Elder Abuse 61

Risk Factors and Protective Factors 62

Promoting Awareness and Education on Elder Abuse 65

Strengthening Support Networks and Resources in Elder Abuse Prevention 70

Chapter 7 Empowering Older Adults 75

Enhancing Well-being and Quality of Life 76

Encouraging Self-Advocacy and Independence 80

The Significance of Social Connections and Engagement 84

Chapter 8 Building a Safer Future 89

The Significance of Building a Safer Future 89

Prevention of Social Isolation 90

Policy Recommendations and Legislative Changes 93

Collaboration and Community Initiatives 97

Chapter 9 Healing and Recovery 103

The Significance of Healing and Recovery:Healing and recovery are crucial for several reasons 103

Trauma-Informed Care for Elder Abuse Survivors 107

Therapeutic Approaches and Support Services for Elder Abuse Survivors 111

Chapter 10 Global Perspectives on Elder Abuse 117

Prevalence and Forms of Elder Abuse 117

Cross-cultural Perspectives and Challenges in Addressing Elder Abuse 120

Creating a World Free from Elder Abuse 124

Conclusion 128

Introduction

Elder abuse is a grave societal issue that demands our attention and concerted efforts to protect and support older adults. This book, titled "Unseen Wounds: Understanding and Addressing Elder Abuse," serves as a comprehensive guide to shed light on the hidden epidemic of elder abuse, providing valuable insights, knowledge, and strategies to combat this pervasive problem. By exploring the various dimensions of elder abuse, its impact on individuals and society, and the interventions and preventive measures available, this book aims to empower readers to make a positive difference in the lives of older adults.

The title "Unseen Wounds" encapsulates the hidden nature of elder abuse, as the wounds inflicted upon older adults are often invisible to society. Elder abuse occurs behind closed doors, within families, caregiving relationships, and communities, leaving lasting scars on the lives of older adults. The purpose of this book is to bring these wounds into the spotlight, raise awareness, and inspire action to create a world where elder abuse is not tolerated.

The book takes a comprehensive approach to understanding elder abuse, encompassing various forms of mistreatment, including physical, emotional, financial, and neglect. Through the exploration of case studies, research findings, and expert insights, readers will gain a deep understanding of the dynamics, prevalence, and consequences of elder abuse. By illuminating the multifaceted aspects of elder abuse, readers will be equipped with the knowledge to recognize, respond to, and prevent abuse in their own lives and communities.

Recognizing that elder abuse is a complex issue influenced by social, cultural, and economic factors, this book delves into the root causes and contributing factors that perpetuate mistreatment of older adults. By examining the broader social context, readers will gain insights into the interplay of ageism, caregiver stress, financial strain, social isolation, and other determinants that exacerbate the vulnerability of older adults to abuse.

Moreover, this book highlights the importance of early intervention and support for elder abuse survivors. By examining the impact of abuse on the physical and emotional well-being of older adults, readers will understand the urgent need for effective support services that address the long-lasting consequences of mistreatment. Trauma-informed care, counseling, support groups, and access to resources are explored as essential components of the healing and recovery process for elder abuse survivors.

In addition to addressing the immediate needs of survivors, this book also emphasizes the critical role of prevention in combating elder abuse. By exploring strategies to raise awareness, promote education, and foster a culture of respect for older adults, readers will be inspired to take proactive steps in their communities and institutions to prevent abuse from occurring in the first place. From empowering caregivers to creating age-friendly environments, the book offers practical approaches to creating a supportive and abuse-free society for older adults.

Recognizing that elder abuse is not confined to a specific region or culture, this book takes a global perspective on the issue. By exploring cross-cultural perspectives and examining the challenges faced by different societies in addressing elder abuse, readers will gain a nuanced understanding of the cultural contexts that shape the dynamics of mistreatment. This cross-cultural lens fosters appreciation for diversity and informs the development of culturally sensitive strategies to combat elder abuse effectively.

"Unseen Wounds: Understanding and Addressing Elder Abuse" is a comprehensive resource that aims to shed light on the hidden epidemic of elder abuse. By providing insights into the various forms of abuse, the contributing factors, the impact on older adults, and the strategies for prevention and intervention, this book equips readers with the knowledge and tools to take action. It is a call to society, individuals, communities, organizations, and policymakers to prioritize the well-being and rights of older adults and create a world where elder abuse is not tolerated. Together, we can bring these unseen wounds into the light, support survivors, and work towards a future where older adults are protected, respected, and valued.

CHAPTER 1
Defining Elder Abuse

Elder abuse is a distressing and pervasive issue that demands our attention and understanding. In this chapter, we embark on a comprehensive exploration of elder abuse, aiming to provide a clear definition and understanding of its various forms. By defining elder abuse and examining its manifestations, we lay the groundwork for recognizing and addressing this grave problem.

Elder abuse encompasses a range of harmful actions or omissions that cause harm, distress, or suffering to older adults. It is a violation of human rights and a betrayal of trust, with devastating consequences for its victims. Understanding the different types of elder abuse is crucial for recognizing its presence and taking appropriate action.

Types of Elder Abuse

Elder abuse encompasses a range of harmful actions or omissions that cause harm, distress, or suffering to older adults. To effectively address this pressing issue, it is crucial to understand the various types of elder abuse that exist. In this chapter, we will delve into the different forms of elder abuse, examining their characteristics, indicators, and the profound impact they have on the lives of older adults.

Physical Abuse

Physical abuse involves the intentional use of force that results in pain, injury, or impairment to an older adult. It may manifest through actions such as hitting, slapping, pushing, or restraining. Perpetrators may resort to physical abuse as a means of exerting control or venting frustration. Older adults who experience physical abuse often bear visible signs such as bruises, fractures, lacerations, or sprains. In some cases, these injuries may be explained away or hidden, making detection challenging.

Emotional and Psychological Abuse

Emotional and psychological abuse inflict mental pain, anguish, or distress upon older adults through verbal or non-verbal means. This form of abuse can take various forms, including humiliation, ridicule, insults, threats, intimidation, or isolating the individual from social interactions. Perpetrators may demean the older adult's self-worth, manipulate their emotions, or undermine their confidence. Emotional and psychological abuse often leaves no visible marks, making it difficult to detect. However, its impact on the mental and emotional well-being of older adults can be severe, leading to depression, anxiety, withdrawal, or a diminished sense of self.

Financial Exploitation

Financial exploitation involves the unauthorized or improper use of an older adult's financial resources for personal gain. Perpetrators may manipulate or deceive older adults into providing access to their financial assets or exploit their vulnerability to gain control over their finances. This can include stealing money, forging signatures, coercing changes in wills or property deeds, or using undue influence to manipulate financial decisions. Signs of financial exploitation may include sudden or unexplained changes in financial status, missing funds, unaccounted withdrawals, or unauthorized use of credit cards. The impact of financial exploitation extends beyond the loss of money and assets, often eroding trust, security, and independence for older adults.

Neglect

Neglect occurs when a caregiver or responsible individual fails to provide the necessary care, support, or attention required to meet the basic needs of an older adult. It can manifest in various ways, including the failure to provide adequate food, water, clothing, shelter, hygiene, medical care, or emotional support. Neglect can result from intentional disregard or due to the caregiver's inability to fulfill their responsibilities adequately. Signs of neglect may include malnutrition, dehydration, poor personal hygiene, untreated medical conditions, hazardous living conditions, or social isolation. Neglect can have severe consequences on the physical, emotional, and overall well-being of older adults, exacerbating existing health conditions and contributing to a decline in their quality of life.

Sexual Abuse

Sexual abuse involves any non-consensual sexual contact or activity imposed on an older adult. This includes unwanted sexual touching, intercourse, coerced nudity, or any form of sexual exploitation. Perpetrators may take advantage of vulnerabilities, including physical or cognitive impairments, to commit sexual abuse. It is crucial to recognize that older adults can experience sexual abuse and that consent is a vital factor in any sexual interaction, regardless of age. Older adults who have experienced sexual abuse may exhibit physical signs of injury or discomfort, changes in behavior, emotional distress, or withdrawal from social interactions.

Understanding the different types of elder abuse is essential for recognizing and addressing this critical issue. Physical abuse, emotional and psychological abuse, financial exploitation, neglect, and sexual abuse are all forms of mistreatment that older

Recognizing the Signs of Elder Abuse

Elder abuse is a distressing reality that often occurs behind closed doors, making it crucial to recognize the signs and indicators. Identifying elder abuse is a complex process that requires awareness, observation, and a deep understanding of the various forms of mistreatment older adults may experience. In this chapter, we will explore the signs of elder abuse, paying attention to physical, behavioral, emotional, and environmental indicators. By familiarizing ourselves with these signs, we can play a vital role in intervening and protecting older adults from further harm.

Physical Indicators

Physical indicators of elder abuse may include visible signs of injury or neglect. These can range from unexplained bruises, welts, or burns to fractures, sprains, or other injuries inconsistent with the explanation provided. Caregivers or family members may attempt to conceal injuries by keeping the older adult isolated or providing implausible explanations for the marks. Poor hygiene, malnutrition, dehydration, weight loss, or untreated medical conditions are also physical signs that may suggest neglect or abuse.

Behavioral Indicators

Behavioral changes can be significant indicators of elder abuse. Older adults who are being abused may exhibit fear, anxiety, or agitation in the presence of certain individuals, particularly caregivers or family members. They may become withdrawn, emotionally distant, or socially isolated. Unexplained changes in mood or personality, such as sudden shifts from being outgoing to exhibiting depression or anxiety, should also raise concerns. Other behavioral indicators may include sleep disturbances, unexplained changes in appetite, or self-soothing behaviors like rocking or mumbling.

Emotional Indicators

Elder abuse takes a toll on the emotional well-being of older adults. Emotional indicators may include expressions of fear, sadness, helplessness, or hopelessness. Older adults who experience abuse may display signs of low self-esteem, shame, or guilt, often blaming themselves for the mistreatment they endure. They may become overly submissive or excessively dependent on their abusers. Additionally, the sudden loss of interest in activities they once enjoyed, reluctance to communicate openly, or expressions of fear towards certain individuals may signal emotional abuse.

Environmental Indicators

The environment in which older adults reside can also provide valuable clues regarding possible elder abuse. Signs of neglect or inadequate care may be evident in unsanitary living conditions, cluttered or unsafe environments, lack of necessary medical equipment or assistive devices, or insufficient heating or cooling. The absence of essential amenities or limited access to food, water, or medication can also indicate neglect or financial exploitation.

Recognizing Patterns and Context

It is important to consider the patterns and context surrounding the observed indicators. Isolated incidents may warrant investigation, but it is often the repetition or clustering of indicators that raises significant concerns. Contextual factors such as the relationship dynamics between the older adult and their caregiver or family member, any history of violence or conflict, or the presence of substance abuse issues can provide additional insight into the potential presence of elder abuse.

Challenges in Recognizing Elder Abuse

Recognizing elder abuse can be challenging due to various factors. Older adults may be reluctant to disclose abuse due to fear, shame, or a sense of loyalty towards their abuser. Cognitive impairments or communication difficulties can further hinder their ability to articulate their experiences. Language barriers or cultural norms may affect the willingness of older adults to seek help or report abuse. Additionally, caregivers or family members who perpetrate the abuse may employ tactics of manipulation, coercion, or intimidation to prevent detection.

Recognizing the signs of elder abuse is crucial for protecting the well-being of older adults. By paying attention to physical, behavioral, emotional, and environmental indicators, we can identify potential cases of mistreatment. It is essential to approach this process with sensitivity, empathy, and respect, ensuring that older adults feel heard, supported, and empowered to disclose their experiences. Recognizing the signs of elder abuse is the first step towards intervention, advocacy, and creating a safe environment for older adults to thrive.

Chapter 2

Understanding the Impact of Elder Abuse

Elder abuse inflicts significant harm on older adults, affecting their physical, emotional, and psychological well-being. To address this grave issue effectively, it is essential to comprehend the profound impact that elder abuse has on its victims. In this chapter, we will explore the consequences of elder abuse and the long-lasting effects it can have on older adults' health, relationships, and overall quality of life. By gaining a comprehensive understanding of these impacts, we can advocate for prevention, support survivors, and work towards creating a society that protects and values its aging population.

Physical Impact

Physical abuse can cause immediate and long-term physical consequences for older adults. The physical injuries resulting from abuse may range from minor bruises and cuts to more severe conditions such as fractures, head trauma, or internal injuries. These injuries can lead to chronic pain, reduced mobility, or disabilities that affect the older adult's ability to perform daily activities independently. Additionally, physical abuse can exacerbate existing health conditions or contribute to the development of new medical issues, leading to a decline in overall health and well-being.

Emotional and Psychological Impact

Elder abuse takes a heavy toll on the emotional and psychological well-being of older adults. The experience of abuse can lead to feelings of fear, anxiety, and mistrust. Survivors may suffer from depression, post-traumatic stress disorder (PTSD), or other mental health conditions. The emotional trauma of abuse can erode an older adult's self-esteem, leading to a diminished sense of self-worth and confidence. They may experience a loss of interest in activities they once enjoyed, withdraw from social interactions, or develop a heightened sense of vulnerability.

Cognitive Impact

Elder abuse can have a detrimental impact on cognitive functioning, particularly in cases of repeated or chronic abuse. The stress and trauma associated with abuse can contribute to cognitive decline and increase the risk of developing conditions such as dementia or Alzheimer's disease. Older adults who experience abuse may exhibit difficulties with memory, attention, decision-making, or problem-solving. These cognitive impairments can further compromise their independence and overall quality of life.

Social Impact

Elder abuse can lead to social isolation and strained relationships with family, friends, and caregivers. Survivors may feel ashamed, embarrassed, or reluctant to disclose their experiences, leading to a withdrawal from social interactions. The fear of judgment or reprisal can prevent older adults from seeking support or sharing their struggles with others. Furthermore, the loss of trust in caregivers or family members can strain existing relationships and create barriers to accessing care and support.

Financial Impact

Financial exploitation can have devastating consequences for older adults, impacting their financial stability and security. Older adults who experience financial abuse may suffer significant financial losses, depleting their savings, retirement funds, or assets. This loss of financial resources can result in an increased dependence on others, limited access to essential needs such as healthcare or medication, and a diminished ability to maintain a comfortable standard of living. The financial impact of abuse can perpetuate a cycle of vulnerability and exacerbate the emotional and psychological distress experienced by survivors.

Long-Term Consequences

The effects of elder abuse are not confined to the immediate aftermath but can have long-term consequences. Survivors may continue to experience physical, emotional, or psychological symptoms long after the abuse has ended. The trauma of abuse can leave a lasting impact on an older adult's overall well-being, leading to chronic health conditions, ongoing mental health challenges, and diminished quality of life. The long-term consequences of elder abuse highlight the need for comprehensive support services and interventions that address the complex needs of survivors.

Understanding the impact of elder abuse is crucial for addressing the needs of survivors and developing effective strategies for prevention and intervention. The physical, emotional, cognitive, social, and financial impacts of elder abuse underscore the urgency of combating this grave issue. By acknowledging the far-reaching consequences of elder abuse, we can foster a society that promotes the dignity, safety, and well-being of older adults. Through education, awareness, and supportive measures, we can work towards eradicating elder abuse and creating a world where older adults can age with respect and dignity.

Physical, Emotional, and Psychological Effects of Elder Abuse

Elder abuse inflicts not only physical harm but also profound emotional and psychological distress on its victims. Understanding the specific effects of elder abuse is crucial for recognizing the impact it has on older adults and developing appropriate interventions and support systems. In this chapter, we will explore the physical, emotional, and psychological effects of elder abuse, shedding light on the long-lasting consequences that survivors may experience. By gaining a comprehensive understanding of these effects, we can advocate for prevention, support survivors, and work towards a society that safeguards its aging population.

Physical Effects

Physical abuse can have immediate and long-term physical effects on older adults. The physical harm inflicted through acts of violence or neglect may result in bruises, cuts, fractures, or more severe injuries. Physical abuse can lead to chronic pain, reduced mobility, and physical disabilities that impact an older adult's ability to carry out daily activities independently. The resulting physical impairments can contribute to a decline in overall health and well-being, further compromising the quality of life of older adults. In some cases, physical abuse can even lead to life-threatening injuries or fatalities.

Emotional Effects

Elder abuse takes a significant toll on the emotional well-being of older adults. Survivors of abuse often experience a range of intense and complex emotions, including fear, anxiety, sadness, anger, and helplessness. The emotional trauma of abuse can erode an older adult's self-esteem, self-worth, and confidence. They may develop a deep mistrust of others, particularly caregivers or family members, and may struggle with feelings of shame or guilt. Emotional effects of elder abuse can lead to a loss of interest in previously enjoyed activities, social withdrawal, and feelings of isolation. These emotional consequences can have a profound impact on an older adult's mental health and overall sense of well-being.

Psychological Effects

Elder abuse can cause severe psychological distress, leaving long-lasting effects on survivors. The experience of abuse can contribute to the development or exacerbation of mental health conditions such as depression, anxiety disorders, post-traumatic stress disorder (PTSD), or suicidal ideation. Older adults who have endured abuse may constantly live in fear, anticipating further harm or retribution. They may experience flashbacks or intrusive thoughts related to the abuse, leading to ongoing psychological trauma. The psychological effects of elder abuse can disrupt an individual's ability to trust others, form new relationships, and navigate daily life with a sense of safety and security.

Complex Interplay of Physical, Emotional, and Psychological Effects

It is important to recognize that the physical, emotional, and psychological effects of elder abuse are interconnected and can reinforce one another. For instance, physical injuries resulting from abuse can trigger emotional distress and psychological trauma. Conversely, the emotional and psychological effects of abuse, such as anxiety or depression, can manifest as physical symptoms such as headaches, gastrointestinal issues, or sleep disturbances. The complex interplay of these effects can have a cumulative negative impact on an older adult's overall health and well-being.

Unique Vulnerabilities and Resilience

It is important to note that older adults may vary in their vulnerability to the physical, emotional, and psychological effects of elder abuse. Factors such as pre-existing health conditions, cognitive abilities, social support networks, and personal resilience can influence an individual's ability to cope with and recover from the effects of abuse. Some older adults may demonstrate remarkable resilience in the face of adversity, while others may experience more profound and long-lasting consequences. Understanding these individual differences can inform tailored interventions and support services to meet the unique needs of survivors.

Importance of Comprehensive Support Services

Given the multifaceted effects of elder abuse, comprehensive support services are crucial in assisting survivors in their journey towards healing and recovery. Physical health care providers can address the immediate medical needs resulting from abuse, while mental health professionals can offer therapeutic interventions to address the emotional and psychological trauma. Social support networks, such as support groups or counseling services, play a vital role in providing survivors with a safe space to share their experiences, receive validation, and connect with others who have faced similar challenges. Rehabilitation services, including physical therapy and occupational therapy, can aid in the recovery of physical function and mobility.

Elder abuse has wide-ranging physical, emotional, and psychological effects on its victims. By recognizing the unique challenges faced by survivors, we can work towards implementing comprehensive support systems that address their diverse needs. Through a holistic approach that combines medical care, mental health support, and social services, we can support older adults in healing from the physical and emotional wounds of abuse. It is our collective responsibility to create a society that prioritizes the well-being and safety of its aging population, fostering an environment where elder abuse has no place.

Long-Term Consequences on Health and Well-being

The impact of elder abuse extends far beyond immediate physical and psychological harm. Older adults who have experienced abuse often face long-term consequences that affect their health, well-being, and overall quality of life. In this chapter, we will explore the enduring effects of elder abuse on the physical and mental health of survivors. By understanding these long-term consequences, we can advocate for prevention, support survivors, and work towards building a society that prioritizes the safety and dignity of older adults.

Physical Health Consequences

Elder abuse can have significant long-term implications for the physical health of survivors. The physical injuries inflicted during episodes of abuse, such as fractures, head trauma, or internal injuries, can lead to chronic pain, mobility issues, and physical disabilities. Older adults may experience a decline in their overall physical functioning, limiting their ability to carry out daily activities independently. Additionally, the stress and trauma associated with abuse can weaken the immune system, making survivors more susceptible to infections, illnesses, and exacerbations of existing health conditions. The long-term physical health consequences of elder abuse can result in a decreased quality of life, increased healthcare utilization, and a higher risk of mortality.

Mental Health Consequences

Elder abuse takes a significant toll on the mental health and well-being of survivors. The emotional and psychological trauma associated with abuse can contribute to the development or worsening of mental health conditions such as depression, anxiety disorders, post-traumatic stress disorder (PTSD), and suicidal ideation. Survivors may experience persistent feelings of fear, anxiety, and helplessness, impacting their ability to trust others and engage in social activities. The long-term psychological consequences of elder abuse can lead to social isolation, cognitive decline, and a diminished sense of self-worth and independence. These mental health challenges further exacerbate the overall impact on an older adult's well-being and can significantly impair their quality of life.

Social Consequences

Elder abuse can have profound social consequences for survivors. The experience of abuse can strain relationships with family members, friends, and caregivers. Survivors may feel ashamed, embarrassed, or reluctant to disclose their experiences, leading to social withdrawal and a sense of isolation. The loss of trust in others can make it challenging for survivors to form new relationships or seek support. The social consequences of elder abuse can further compound feelings of loneliness, negatively impacting an older adult's mental and physical health. Additionally, the stigma surrounding abuse may prevent survivors from accessing the necessary support services and resources available to them.

Financial Consequences

Financial exploitation, a form of elder abuse, can have long-lasting financial consequences for older adults. Survivors may experience significant financial losses, depleting their savings, retirement funds, or assets. The loss of financial resources can lead to increased financial dependency, limited access to essential needs such as healthcare or medication, and a reduced ability to maintain a comfortable standard of living. Financial abuse can perpetuate a cycle of vulnerability, contributing to ongoing financial stress and insecurity for survivors. These financial consequences further exacerbate the overall impact on an older adult's well-being and may compromise their ability to age with dignity and independence.

Overall Quality of Life

The long-term consequences of elder abuse, encompassing physical, mental, social, and financial aspects, can significantly diminish an older adult's overall quality of life. Survivors may experience a reduced sense of autonomy, loss of self-esteem, and diminished enjoyment of daily activities. The trauma and ongoing effects of abuse can erode an individual's sense of safety, trust, and well-being. The long-term consequences on the quality of life underscore the urgent need for comprehensive support services, interventions, and policy measures to prevent and address elder abuse effectively.

Elder abuse has enduring consequences on the health, well-being, and overall quality of life of survivors. The physical, mental, social, and financial impacts of abuse can persist long after the abuse has occurred, posing significant challenges for older adults as they navigate their daily lives. By recognizing and understanding these long-term consequences, we can advocate for prevention efforts, provide comprehensive support services, and promote a society that values and safeguards its aging population. It is essential that we work collectively to raise awareness, support survivors, and ensure that older adults are able to age with dignity, respect, and the highest possible quality of life.

Chapter 3
Exploring the Factors Contributing to Elder Abuse

To effectively address elder abuse, it is crucial to understand the factors that contribute to its occurrence. Elder abuse is a complex issue influenced by various individual, interpersonal, and societal factors. In this chapter, we will explore the underlying factors that contribute to elder abuse, including social isolation and loneliness, caregiver stress and burnout, and financial strain and exploitation. By examining these factors, we can develop targeted interventions and preventive strategies to mitigate the risk of elder abuse and create a safer environment for older adults.

Caregiver Stress and Burnout

Caregiver stress and burnout are critical factors that contribute to elder abuse. Caregivers, whether family members or professionals, often face numerous challenges and responsibilities in caring for older adults. The demands of caregiving can be physically, emotionally, and financially overwhelming, leading to high levels of stress and burnout. Caregivers experiencing stress and burnout may become resentful, frustrated, or unable to cope effectively. These negative emotions can increase the likelihood of elder abuse, as caregivers may engage in abusive behaviors due to their own unmet needs, exhaustion, or feelings of helplessness.

Financial Strain and Exploitation

Financial strain and exploitation are significant risk factors for elder abuse. Older adults who are financially dependent or experience financial difficulties may be vulnerable to exploitation by caregivers, family members, or strangers seeking to take advantage of their resources. Financial exploitation can take various forms, including theft, fraud, coercion, or undue influence. Perpetrators may manipulate older adults into giving them money, assets, or access to financial accounts. Older adults who experience financial strain may also face increased pressure to provide financial support to family members, exacerbating their vulnerability to exploitation.

Cognitive Impairment and Dependency

Cognitive impairments, such as dementia or Alzheimer's disease, can contribute to the occurrence of elder abuse. Older adults with cognitive impairments may have difficulty making sound judgments, recognizing abusive situations, or articulating their experiences. Their dependency on caregivers for daily activities, decision-making, and financial management can create power imbalances and increase the risk of abuse. Caregivers may exploit the cognitive vulnerabilities of older adults, leading to neglect, financial exploitation, or other forms of mistreatment.

Cultural and Societal Factors

Cultural and societal factors can also contribute to elder abuse. Cultural norms, beliefs, and attitudes towards aging, family dynamics, and gender roles can influence the prevalence and acceptance of abuse within certain communities. Language barriers, discrimination, or lack of awareness about elder abuse can further impede the detection and prevention of mistreatment. Societal factors such as inadequate support systems, limited resources, or ineffective legal frameworks may also contribute to the perpetuation of elder abuse.

Prevention and Intervention Strategies

To address the factors contributing to elder abuse, comprehensive prevention and intervention strategies are crucial. Increasing social connectedness and combating social isolation through community programs, support groups, and volunteer initiatives can reduce the risk of elder abuse. Providing respite care and support services for caregivers can alleviate stress and prevent burnout. Financial education and protection measures can empower older adults to make informed decisions and safeguard their financial resources. Awareness campaigns, training programs, and policy initiatives that address cultural and societal factors can help shift attitudes, promote respectful aging, and create a society that values and protects its older adults.

Exploring the factors contributing to elder abuse reveals the complex web of individual, interpersonal, and societal influences that contribute to its occurrence. Social isolation and loneliness, caregiver stress and burnout, financial strain and exploitation, cognitive impairments, and cultural/societal factors all play significant roles in shaping the landscape of elder abuse. By understanding these contributing factors, we can develop targeted interventions, promote awareness, and implement preventive strategies that mitigate the risk of elder abuse. It is essential that we work collectively to foster a society that supports and protects its aging population, ensuring that older adults can age with dignity, safety, and respect.

Social Isolation and Loneliness in Relation to Elder Abuse

Social isolation and loneliness are significant factors that contribute to elder abuse, highlighting the crucial role of social connections in safeguarding the well-being of older adults. In this chapter, we will delve into the causes and consequences of social isolation and loneliness among older adults, explore their relationship with elder abuse, and discuss strategies to address and prevent these issues. By understanding the impact of social isolation and loneliness, we can work towards creating a society that values social connectedness and supports older adults in maintaining meaningful relationships.

Causes of Social Isolation and Loneliness

Social isolation and loneliness among older adults can stem from various factors. The loss of a spouse or close family members, retirement, geographic separation from loved ones, limited mobility, and health conditions can contribute to social isolation. Changes in social roles and networks, such as children moving away or friends passing away, can disrupt social connections. Ageism and societal attitudes that devalue older adults can also lead to social exclusion. Additionally, barriers such as transportation difficulties, financial constraints, and lack of access to community resources can further exacerbate social isolation.

Consequences of Social Isolation and Loneliness

Social isolation and loneliness have detrimental effects on the physical, emotional, and mental well-being of older adults. Without regular social interactions, older adults may experience a decline in physical health, including higher rates of chronic conditions, compromised immune function, and increased mortality risk. Loneliness has been linked to higher rates of depression, anxiety, cognitive decline, and overall decreased life satisfaction. Furthermore, social isolation and loneliness can impact an older adult's self-esteem, sense of belonging, and quality of life, leading to a diminished sense of purpose and fulfillment.

Relationship between Social Isolation, Loneliness, and Elder Abuse

Social isolation and loneliness are closely linked to the occurrence of elder abuse. Older adults who lack social connections and support systems are more vulnerable to abuse and exploitation. Isolated individuals may become more dependent on caregivers or family members, creating an imbalance of power and increasing the risk of mistreatment. Loneliness can also make older adults more susceptible to manipulation, as they may seek companionship and connection, making them targets for perpetrators who exploit their vulnerability.

Isolation and abuse can form a vicious cycle, as the experience of abuse further isolates older adults, eroding their trust and willingness to seek help. Shame and fear of judgment may prevent them from disclosing abuse or reaching out for support. The silence resulting from social isolation can perpetuate abuse, making it crucial to address both the causes and consequences of social isolation and loneliness as part of preventing elder abuse.

Prevention and Intervention Strategies

Addressing social isolation and loneliness is essential for the prevention of elder abuse. Implementing preventive strategies can foster social connectedness and reduce the risk of mistreatment. Some effective approaches include:

Community Programs

1. Establishing community-based programs that encourage social participation, such as senior centers, clubs, and intergenerational activities, can provide older adults with opportunities for social engagement and companionship.

Volunteer Initiatives

2. Encouraging volunteerism among older adults allows them to contribute to their communities, form new connections, and combat feelings of social isolation.

Technology and Digital Inclusion

3. Promoting digital literacy and access to technology can enable older adults to connect with others online, participate in virtual communities, and maintain social ties, even when physical interactions are limited.

Transportation and Accessibility

4. Improving transportation options and accessibility to community services can facilitate older adults' participation in social activities and reduce barriers to engagement.

Supportive Housing and Aging-in-Place Initiatives

5. Creating age-friendly environments that prioritize community integration and support independent living can help older adults maintain social connections within their own neighborhoods.

Caregiver Support

6. Providing resources, respite care, and support services for caregivers can alleviate their burden, reduce stress, and prevent caregiver burnout, thus improving the overall quality of care provided to older adults.

Education and Awareness

Raising awareness about the importance of social connections, the signs of social isolation and loneliness, and the risks of elder abuse can help communities identify and intervene in situations of vulnerability.

Social isolation and loneliness have detrimental effects on the well-being of older adults and significantly contribute to the risk of elder abuse. Recognizing the causes and consequences of social isolation and loneliness is crucial for developing effective preventive strategies. By fostering social connections, creating supportive environments, and implementing caregiver support programs, we can reduce social isolation and loneliness among older adults, enhance their quality of life, and create a safer and more inclusive society. It is our collective responsibility to prioritize social connectedness and ensure that older adults are valued, respected, and supported in maintaining meaningful relationships.

Caregiver Stress and Burnout in Relation to Elder Abuse

Caregivers play a vital role in supporting the well-being and independence of older adults. However, the demanding nature of caregiving can lead to significant stress and burnout. In this chapter, we will explore the causes and consequences of caregiver stress and burnout, examine their relationship to elder abuse, and discuss strategies to address and prevent these issues. By understanding the impact of caregiver stress and burnout, we can support caregivers and create a healthier caregiving environment that promotes the well-being of both caregivers and older adults.

Causes of Caregiver Stress and Burnout

Caregiver stress and burnout can arise from various factors associated with the caregiving role. The physical demands of providing care, such as assisting with personal hygiene, managing medications, or supporting mobility, can be physically exhausting. Emotional challenges, such as witnessing the decline of a loved one's health, coping with behavioral changes, or dealing with end-of-life issues, can take a toll on a caregiver's mental well-being. The time commitment and loss of personal freedom or career opportunities can create a sense of isolation and sacrifice. Financial strain, lack of social support, and limited access to respite care or support services can further contribute to caregiver stress and burnout.

Consequences of Caregiver Stress and Burnout

Caregiver stress and burnout have significant consequences for both caregivers and the older adults they care for. Caregivers experiencing high levels of stress and burnout are more prone to physical and mental health issues. They may experience fatigue, sleep disturbances, compromised immune function, and an increased risk of chronic conditions. Mental health challenges, such as depression, anxiety, and caregiver-specific stressors, can further impair a caregiver's well-being and ability to provide effective care. Additionally, caregiver stress and burnout can strain relationships with family members, friends, and the care recipient, potentially leading to conflict and emotional distress for all parties involved.

Relationship between Caregiver Stress, Burnout, and Elder Abuse

Caregiver stress and burnout are closely linked to the occurrence of elder abuse. High levels of stress can impair a caregiver's judgment, patience, and emotional regulation, increasing the risk of engaging in abusive behaviors. Caregivers experiencing burnout may feel overwhelmed, emotionally drained, and detached from their role, leading to a lack of empathy or neglect. The demands of caregiving combined with the caregiver's own unmet needs, exhaustion, or feelings of helplessness can contribute to abusive behaviors, such as physical, emotional, or financial mistreatment of the older adult. Additionally, the strain of caregiving may lead to increased reliance on negative coping mechanisms, such as substance abuse, further heightening the risk of abuse.

Prevention and Intervention Strategies

1. Addressing caregiver stress and burnout is crucial for the prevention of elder abuse and the well-being of both caregivers and older adults. Implementing preventive strategies and interventions can help alleviate caregiver stress and promote a healthier caregiving environment. Some effective approaches include:

Respite Care

2. Providing respite care services that offer temporary relief to caregivers can reduce their stress and provide an opportunity for self-care and rejuvenation.

Support Services

3. Offering support services, such as counseling, support groups, or helplines, specifically tailored to caregivers, can provide emotional support, education, and coping strategies.

Education and Training

4. Providing caregivers with education and training on effective caregiving techniques, communication skills, and self-care

strategies can enhance their confidence and reduce stress levels.

Financial Assistance

5. Offering financial assistance or resources to alleviate the financial strain associated with caregiving, such as reimbursement for caregiving expenses or access to financial planning support, can mitigate one of the major stressors for caregivers.

Resilience-Building

6. ProgramsImplementing resilience-building programs that focus on stress management techniques, self-care practices, and fostering social support networks can enhance caregiver well-being and promote healthier coping mechanisms.

Collaboration with Healthcare Professionals

7. Encouraging collaboration between caregivers and healthcare professionals can facilitate coordinated care, provide support, and ensure that caregivers have access to necessary resources and information.

Caregiver stress and burnout pose significant risks to both caregivers and the older adults they care for, highlighting the importance of addressing these issues in the context of elder abuse prevention. By recognizing the causes and consequences of caregiver stress and burnout, we can implement effective strategies that support caregivers and create a healthier caregiving environment. Providing respite care, support services, education and training, financial assistance, and resilience-building programs can help alleviate caregiver stress, reduce the risk of burnout, and promote the well-being of both caregivers and older adults. It is essential that we prioritize the support of caregivers, recognize their invaluable contributions, and work towards creating a caregiving environment that promotes the safety, dignity, and well-being of older adults.

Financial Strain and Exploitation in Relation to Elder Abuse

Financial strain and exploitation are significant factors that contribute to elder abuse, highlighting the vulnerability of older adults when it comes to their financial well-being. In this chapter, we will explore the causes and consequences of financial strain and exploitation among older adults, examine their relationship with elder abuse, and discuss strategies to address and prevent these issues. By understanding the impact of financial strain and exploitation, we can work towards creating a society that safeguards the financial security and dignity of older adults.

Causes of Financial Strain

Financial strain among older adults can stem from various factors. Retirement, reduced income, increased healthcare expenses, and inadequate savings can create financial challenges. Rising costs of living, inflation, and limited access to affordable housing or essential resources further exacerbate financial strain. Older adults may also face financial difficulties due to the loss of a spouse or partner, lack of access to pensions or retirement benefits, or insufficient social security income. Economic downturns or unexpected expenses can further contribute to financial strain, leaving older adults vulnerable to exploitation.

Forms of Financial Exploitation

1. Financial exploitation involves the unauthorized or improper use of an older adult's financial resources for personal gain. It can take various forms, including:

Theft and Fraud

2. Perpetrators may steal money, possessions, or valuable assets from older adults through theft, deception, or scams.

Coercion and Undue Influence

3. Manipulative individuals exert control over an older adult's decision-making, pressuring them into making financial transactions, changing wills, or granting power of attorney.

Deceptive Sales Practices

4. Older adults may be targeted by unscrupulous salespeople who use aggressive or misleading tactics to persuade them into purchasing unnecessary or overpriced products or services.

Caregiver Exploitation

5. Caregivers, family members, or trusted individuals may exploit their relationship with an older adult to gain access to their financial resources, misuse their funds, or manipulate financial decision-making.

Consequences of Financial Strain and Exploitation

Financial strain and exploitation have significant consequences for the well-being and quality of life of older adults. The loss of financial resources can result in decreased financial security, limited access to essential needs such as healthcare, medication, or nutritious food, and an increased reliance on others for financial support. Financial exploitation can cause emotional distress, erode trust in others, and lead to feelings of shame, guilt, or vulnerability. Older adults who experience financial strain and exploitation may also face long-term financial repercussions, including depleted savings, reduced quality of life, and increased dependency on public assistance programs.

Relationship between Financial Strain, Exploitation, and Elder Abuse

Financial strain and exploitation are closely linked to the occurrence of elder abuse. Older adults experiencing financial difficulties or relying on others for financial support may be more vulnerable to exploitation and manipulation. Perpetrators often target individuals who appear financially desperate or lack knowledge about their rights and financial management. The power dynamics associated with financial dependence can increase an older adult's susceptibility to coercion, undue influence, or deceptive practices. Financial exploitation can lead to a range of abusive behaviors, including neglect, physical or emotional abuse, and isolation.

Prevention and Intervention Strategies

Addressing financial strain and exploitation is crucial for the prevention of elder abuse and the protection of older adults' financial well-being. Implementing preventive strategies and interventions can help mitigate the risk of financial exploitation and support the financial security of older adults. Some effective approaches include:

Financial Education and Empowerment

1. Providing older adults with access to financial education programs, resources, and tools can enhance their knowledge, decision-making abilities, and awareness of financial scams and exploitation.

Professional Guidance

2. Encouraging older adults to seek advice from trusted financial professionals, such as financial planners or elder law attorneys, can provide them with guidance on managing their finances, estate planning, and protecting their assets.

Caregiver Support and Monitoring

3. Implementing caregiver support programs that promote ethical behavior, provide training on financial management, and establish monitoring systems can reduce the risk of caregiver exploitation.

Enhanced Legal Protections

4. Strengthening legal protections against financial exploitation, including stricter regulations, penalties for perpetrators, and safeguards for older adults, can act as a deterrent and provide recourse for victims.

Community Awareness and Collaboration

5. Raising community awareness about financial exploitation and fostering collaborations between community organizations, financial institutions, and law enforcement agencies can improve detection, reporting, and response to cases of financial abuse.

Financial strain and exploitation pose significant risks to the well-being and security of older adults, highlighting the importance of addressing these issues in the context of elder abuse prevention. By recognizing the causes and consequences of financial strain and exploitation, we can implement effective strategies to prevent financial abuse, promote financial empowerment, and protect the financial well-being of older adults. Providing financial education, professional guidance, caregiver support, enhanced legal protections, and community collaboration can contribute to a society that safeguards the financial security and dignity of older adults. It is crucial that we prioritize the financial well-being of older adults, ensure their access to resources, and work collectively to prevent financial exploitation and abuse.

CHAPTER 4
Identifying Vulnerable Populations in Relation to Elder Abuse

Identifying vulnerable populations is crucial for understanding the specific risks and challenges they face regarding elder abuse. Certain groups of older adults may be more susceptible to abuse due to factors such as age, health conditions, socioeconomic status, or cultural backgrounds. In this chapter, we will explore various vulnerable populations, examine their unique vulnerabilities to elder abuse, and discuss strategies to protect and support them. By recognizing these vulnerable populations, we can develop targeted interventions, raise awareness, and ensure the well-being of all older adults.

Frail and Dependent Older Adults

Frail and dependent older adults are particularly vulnerable to elder abuse due to their physical limitations and increased dependency on others for daily activities. These individuals may require assistance with personal care, mobility, or medication management, making them reliant on caregivers. Their vulnerability can be further exacerbated if they lack social support networks or are isolated from their communities. Caregivers or family members may exploit their dependence, engaging in abusive behaviors or neglecting their needs.

Individuals with Cognitive Impairments

Older adults with cognitive impairments, such as dementia or Alzheimer's disease, are at heightened risk of elder abuse. Their cognitive limitations may impair their ability to recognize abusive situations, communicate their experiences, or make informed decisions. Caregivers or others may take advantage of their cognitive vulnerabilities, manipulating them for personal gain or engaging in neglectful behaviors. It is crucial to implement safeguards and tailored support services to protect the rights and well-being of individuals with cognitive impairments.

Socially Isolated Older Adults

Social isolation and loneliness increase the risk of elder abuse. Older adults who lack social connections and support systems are more susceptible to mistreatment, as they may be more reliant on caregivers or others who may exploit their vulnerability. Socially isolated older adults may have limited opportunities for social interaction, making it difficult to detect abuse or access necessary support services. Community engagement programs, support groups, and volunteer initiatives can help combat social isolation and protect this vulnerable population.

Marginalized and Underserved Communities

Certain marginalized and underserved communities, including racial and ethnic minorities, immigrant populations, and individuals with limited English proficiency, face unique challenges and vulnerabilities concerning elder abuse. Language barriers, cultural norms, discrimination, and lack of awareness about available resources can hinder their access to support services and appropriate interventions. Tailored outreach efforts, culturally sensitive education, and engagement initiatives can help bridge these gaps and ensure equitable protection for all older adults.

LGBTQ+ Older Adults

LGBTQ+ older adults may face heightened vulnerability to elder abuse due to factors such as stigma, discrimination, and historical lack of legal protections. These individuals may have experienced a lifetime of discrimination, which can impact their physical and mental well-being and limit their access to support networks. Elder abuse in LGBTQ+ communities may occur within families, care settings, or broader society. Culturally competent services, inclusive policies, and supportive environments can help safeguard the rights and well-being of LGBTQ+ older adults.

Older Adults Experiencing Intimate Partner Violence

Intimate partner violence (IPV) can continue into later life, putting older adults at risk of abuse from their current or former partners. Older adults experiencing IPV may face unique challenges in seeking help, such as financial dependence, fear of retaliation, or lack of awareness about available resources. Recognizing the signs of IPV among older adults and providing specialized support services, including safe shelters, counseling, and legal assistance, is crucial to addressing this vulnerable population.

Strategies to Protect Vulnerable Populations

To protect vulnerable populations from elder abuse, a multi-faceted approach is necessary

Education and Awareness

1. Raising awareness about the unique vulnerabilities and challenges faced by different populations is essential. Educational campaigns, training programs, and culturally

sensitive materials can help promote understanding, recognition, and appropriate response to elder abuse within vulnerable populations.

Tailored Interventions

2. Developing targeted interventions that address the specific needs of vulnerable populations is crucial. This may include providing specialized support services, language assistance, cultural sensitivity training, and legal protections that consider the unique circumstances and challenges faced by each group.

Collaboration and Partnerships

3. Establishing collaborations between healthcare providers, social services, community organizations, and advocacy groups can enhance the coordination of care, improve access to resources, and ensure a holistic approach to protecting vulnerable populations.

Empowerment and Advocacy

4. Empowering vulnerable populations by promoting self-advocacy, fostering social connections, and providing resources and tools can help reduce their vulnerability to abuse. Encouraging participation in decision-making, promoting their rights, and amplifying their voices can support their overall well-being and protection.

Identifying vulnerable populations is crucial for effective prevention, detection, and intervention efforts in elder abuse. Understanding the unique vulnerabilities faced by different populations allows us to develop targeted strategies, raise awareness, and implement protective measures to safeguard the well-being of all older adults. By addressing the specific challenges faced by frail and dependent older adults, individuals with cognitive impairments, socially isolated older adults, marginalized and underserved communities, LGBTQ+ older adults, and those experiencing intimate partner violence, we can work towards a society that values and protects the rights and dignity of all older adults. It is our collective responsibility to ensure that vulnerable populations receive the support, resources, and protections they need to age with safety, respect, and dignity.

Dementia and Cognitive Impairment in Relation to Elder Abuse

Dementia and cognitive impairment are significant risk factors for elder abuse, highlighting the vulnerability of older adults who experience cognitive decline. In this chapter, we will explore the causes and consequences of dementia and cognitive impairment, examine their relationship with elder abuse, and discuss strategies to protect and support individuals living with these conditions. By understanding the impact of dementia and cognitive impairment, we can work towards creating a society that promotes the well-being and safety of older adults.

Understanding Dementia and Cognitive Impairment

Dementia is a syndrome characterized by a progressive decline in cognitive function, memory loss, impaired judgment, and changes in behavior and personality. Alzheimer's disease is the most common form of dementia, but there are other types as well, including vascular dementia, Lewy body dementia, and frontotemporal dementia. Cognitive impairment refers to a broader range of cognitive deficits that may not meet the criteria for a dementia diagnosis but still impact an individual's ability to function independently.

Causes and Progression

Dementia and cognitive impairment can have various underlying causes. Alzheimer's disease is associated with the accumulation of beta-amyloid plaques and tau protein tangles in the brain. Vascular dementia results from impaired blood flow to the brain, often due to stroke or other vascular conditions. Other causes include traumatic brain injury, Parkinson's disease, Huntington's disease, and certain infections or metabolic disorders. The progression of dementia and cognitive impairment varies depending on the underlying cause, but it typically involves a gradual decline in cognitive abilities and daily functioning.

Vulnerabilities to Elder Abuse

Individuals living with dementia and cognitive impairment are particularly vulnerable to elder abuse due to their diminished cognitive abilities and increased dependency on others. They may struggle to recognize and understand abusive situations, communicate their experiences, or make informed decisions about their safety and well-being. This vulnerability is further exacerbated by the loss of memory, confusion, and disorientation that can occur with these conditions. Caregivers or others may take advantage of their cognitive vulnerabilities, engaging in abusive behaviors, neglecting their needs, or exploiting their resources.

Forms of Elder Abuse

Elder abuse in the context of dementia and cognitive impairment can take various forms, including

Physical Abuse

1. This involves the use of physical force that results in pain, injury, or impairment. It may include hitting, pushing, restraining, or inappropriate use of medications or physical restraints.

Emotional and Psychological Abuse

2. This form of abuse involves the use of threats, humiliation, intimidation, or manipulation to control or harm an individual's emotional well-being. It can include verbal insults, isolation, withholding affection, or treating them as if they are incompetent.

Neglect

3. Neglect occurs when a caregiver fails to provide necessary care, assistance, or supervision, resulting in harm or risk of harm to the person with dementia or cognitive impairment. This may involve withholding food, medication, hygiene assistance, or necessary medical care.

Financial Exploitation

4. Caregivers, family members, or others may exploit the person's cognitive impairment to gain access to their financial resources, misuse their funds, or manipulate financial decision-making.

Consequences and Impact

Elder abuse in the context of dementia and cognitive impairment has significant consequences for the well-being and quality of life of older adults. It can lead to physical injuries, emotional distress, increased confusion, and heightened behavioral symptoms. The abusive experiences can exacerbate cognitive decline, worsen memory loss, and contribute to increased dependency on caregivers. The loss of trust, safety, and dignity can further compromise the person's overall well-being and potentially accelerate the progression of their cognitive impairment.

Prevention and Intervention Strategies

1. Protecting individuals with dementia and cognitive impairment from elder abuse requires a multi-faceted approach:

Education and Training

2. Caregivers, healthcare professionals, and community members should receive education and training on dementia, cognitive impairment, and elder abuse. This includes recognizing signs of abuse, understanding communication strategies, and learning techniques to create a supportive and safe environment.

Person-Centered Care

3. Adopting person-centered care approaches that respect the autonomy and individual needs of those with dementia or cognitive impairment can help reduce the risk of abuse. This includes involving them in decision-making to the extent possible, promoting dignity, and tailoring care to their preferences.

Support for Caregivers

4. Providing support services for caregivers, such as respite care, counseling, and education on managing challenging behaviors, can help reduce caregiver stress and decrease the likelihood of abusive behaviors.

Collaboration and Communication

5. Encouraging collaboration and effective communication between healthcare providers, caregivers, and social services can enhance detection, reporting, and intervention in cases of elder abuse.

Legal Protections

6. Strengthening legal protections for individuals with dementia and cognitive impairment, including guardianship laws, powers of attorney, and financial oversight mechanisms, can help prevent financial exploitation and ensure their rights and well-being are protected.

Community Support and Resources

7. Creating supportive community networks, providing access to support groups, memory cafés, and social activities tailored for individuals with dementia or cognitive impairment, can help reduce social isolation and promote social engagement.

Dementia and cognitive impairment pose unique challenges for older adults and increase their vulnerability to elder abuse. Understanding the causes, progression, and impact of these conditions is essential for developing strategies to protect and support individuals living with dementia and cognitive impairment. By implementing preventive measures, enhancing caregiver support, promoting person-centered care, and strengthening legal protections, we can create a society that safeguards the well-being and dignity of older adults living with dementia and cognitive impairment. It is our collective responsibility to ensure their safety, respect their autonomy, and provide the necessary support to help them age with dignity and quality of life.

Elderly Individuals with Disabilities in Relation to Elder Abuse

Elderly individuals with disabilities are a vulnerable population that requires specific attention and support to protect them from abuse and ensure their well-being. In this chapter, we will explore the unique challenges faced by elderly individuals with disabilities, examine the relationship between disability and elder abuse, and discuss strategies to promote their safety and enhance their quality of life. By understanding the impact of disability on older adults and addressing their specific needs, we can work towards a society that values and supports the rights and dignity of all individuals, regardless of their abilities.

Understanding Disability in Older Adults

Disability among older adults refers to any condition that impairs physical, cognitive, sensory, or mental functioning, affecting their ability to perform daily activities independently. Disabilities may result from chronic illnesses, injuries, degenerative conditions, or congenital disorders. Common disabilities in older adults include mobility limitations, visual or hearing impairments, cognitive impairments (such as dementia or intellectual disabilities), and mental health conditions. Each disability presents unique challenges that require tailored approaches to support and care.

Vulnerabilities to Elder Abuse

Elderly individuals with disabilities face increased vulnerability to abuse due to a combination of factors. Their disabilities may make it difficult for them to protect themselves, communicate effectively, or recognize abusive situations. Dependence on others for daily activities and care increases their reliance on caregivers, family members, or support systems, creating power imbalances that can be exploited. Limited mobility or sensory impairments may also isolate them socially, making it harder to detect and report instances of abuse. These vulnerabilities make it crucial to implement protective measures and support systems to ensure their safety and well-being.

Prevention and Intervention Strategies

To protect elderly individuals with disabilities from abuse, comprehensive strategies and interventions are necessary

Education and Awareness

1. Raising awareness about the rights and needs of elderly individuals with disabilities and providing education on recognizing and responding to elder abuse is essential. This includes training caregivers, healthcare professionals, and community members to detect signs of abuse and provide appropriate support.

Person-Centered Care

2. Adopting person-centered care approaches that prioritize the autonomy and dignity of individuals with disabilities is crucial. This includes involving them in decision-making, tailoring care to their specific needs and preferences, and promoting their independence and self-expression.

Support Services

3. Providing specialized support services, such as assistive devices, accessibility modifications, personal care assistance, and respite care, can enhance their quality of life and reduce their vulnerability to abuse.

Caregiver Training and Support

4. Offering training programs for caregivers that focus on disability-specific care techniques, communication strategies, and stress management can reduce the risk of abusive behaviors and promote the well-being of both the caregiver and the individual with disabilities.

Accessible Reporting and Support Systems

5. Establishing accessible reporting mechanisms for elder abuse and support systems that cater to the unique needs of individuals with disabilities is crucial. This includes providing communication aids, trained professionals who understand disability-related challenges, and coordination with disability service providers to ensure comprehensive support.

Legal Protections

6. Strengthening legal protections for elderly individuals with disabilities, including legislation against elder abuse, guardianship laws, and powers of attorney, can help prevent abuse and provide recourse for victims.

Elderly individuals with disabilities are a vulnerable population that requires tailored support and protection from abuse. Understanding the unique challenges they face and implementing strategies to address their specific needs are crucial for promoting their safety, dignity, and well-being. By raising awareness, providing person-centered care, offering support services, training caregivers, ensuring accessible reporting systems, and strengthening legal protections, we can create a society that values and protects elderly individuals with disabilities. It is our collective responsibility to support their rights, enhance their quality of life, and ensure that they can age with dignity and respect.

Minority and Underserved Communities in Relation to Elder Abuse

Minority and underserved communities are often disproportionately affected by elder abuse due to various factors, including systemic inequalities, cultural barriers, and limited access to resources. In this chapter, we will explore the unique challenges faced by elderly individuals from minority and underserved communities, examine the relationship between these communities and elder abuse, and discuss strategies to promote their safety and well-being. By understanding the impact of these factors, we can work towards creating a society that values and protects the rights of all older adults, regardless of their backgrounds.

Understanding Minority and Underserved Communities

Minority and underserved communities encompass various groups, including racial and ethnic minorities, immigrant populations, individuals with limited English proficiency, and low-income individuals. These communities often face disparities in healthcare, education, employment, and social services. Cultural norms, language barriers, discrimination, and lack of awareness about available resources further contribute to their vulnerability and limited access to support systems.

Challenges Faced by Minority and Underserved Communities

Minority and underserved communities face specific challenges that increase their vulnerability to elder abuse

Language Barriers

1. Limited English proficiency can hinder communication with healthcare providers, social services, and law enforcement agencies, making it difficult to report abuse or access support. Language barriers may also prevent individuals from fully understanding their rights and available resources.

Cultural Norms and Traditions

2. Cultural norms and traditions may affect perceptions of aging, caregiving, and the reporting of abuse. These factors can create barriers to seeking help or disclosing abuse, as individuals may fear stigma, family dishonor, or retaliation.

Discrimination and Stereotyping

3. Systemic racism, discrimination, and stereotypes can lead to social exclusion, limited access to services, and disparities in healthcare. These factors can contribute to increased vulnerability and reduced support networks, making it more challenging to detect and prevent elder abuse.

Economic Disadvantages

4. Economic disparities, low-income levels, and lack of financial resources can limit access to safe and supportive living environments, quality healthcare, and legal representation. Financial constraints can make it harder for individuals to leave abusive situations or seek assistance.

Forms of Elder Abuse in Minority and Underserved Communities

Elder abuse in minority and underserved communities can take various forms

Physical Abuse

5. Physical abuse may involve acts such as hitting, pushing, or restraining an older adult. Cultural norms or language barriers may make it more challenging to recognize and report such abuse.

Emotional and Psychological Abuse

6. Emotional abuse can include verbal insults, threats, or humiliation. Cultural factors, such as collectivist values or intergenerational dynamics, may perpetuate emotional abuse within families or communities.

Neglect

7. Neglect occurs when caregivers fail to provide necessary care, assistance, or supervision, resulting in harm or risk of harm to the older adult. Limited access to healthcare or support services can contribute to neglect in underserved communities.

Financial Exploitation

8. Financial exploitation involves the misuse or theft of an older adult's financial resources. Scammers or perpetrators may target individuals with limited financial literacy or unfamiliarity with the financial systems in their new country.

Strategies to Support Minority and Underserved Communities

To protect minority and underserved communities from elder abuse, a comprehensive approach is necessary

Cultural Competence

1. Developing cultural competence among service providers, including healthcare professionals, social workers, and law

enforcement personnel, is crucial. This includes understanding cultural norms, traditions, and communication styles to provide appropriate and respectful care.

Language Access

2. Ensuring language access is essential for effective communication and access to services. This includes providing interpretation services, translated materials, and multilingual staff to assist individuals with limited English proficiency.

Community Engagement

3. Engaging community leaders, faith-based organizations, and grassroots initiatives can promote awareness, education, and support networks within minority and underserved communities. Community-driven interventions are more likely to be culturally relevant and effective.

Outreach and Education

4. Conducting targeted outreach and educational campaigns can increase awareness about elder abuse, available resources, and rights within minority and underserved communities. These initiatives should be culturally sensitive and address specific barriers faced by each community.

Collaboration and Partnerships

5. Establishing partnerships between community organizations, social service agencies, healthcare providers, and law enforcement can enhance the coordination of services and improve responses to elder abuse cases.

Legal Protections

6. Strengthening legal protections and policies against elder abuse can help safeguard the rights and well-being of older adults in minority and underserved communities. This includes cultural competency training for legal professionals and ensuring equitable access to justice.

Addressing elder abuse in minority and underserved communities requires a comprehensive and culturally sensitive approach. By understanding the unique challenges faced by these communities, we can develop strategies that promote safety, awareness, and support. Culturally competent care, language access, community engagement, outreach and education, collaboration among service providers, and strengthened legal protections are essential in protecting the rights and well-being of older adults in minority and underserved communities. It is our collective responsibility to ensure that all older adults, regardless of their backgrounds, receive equitable care, respect, and protection from elder abuse.

CHAPTER 5

Reporting Elder Abuse: Legal and Ethical Considerations

Reporting elder abuse is a critical step in protecting older adults from further harm and ensuring their safety and well-being. In this chapter, we will explore the legal and ethical considerations involved in reporting elder abuse. We will examine the legal obligations to report abuse, the ethical responsibilities of professionals and individuals, and the potential challenges and dilemmas that may arise. By understanding the legal and ethical landscape surrounding reporting, we can work towards a society that upholds the rights and protects the vulnerable older adults.

Legal Obligations to Report

Many jurisdictions have laws that impose legal obligations to report elder abuse. These laws vary by jurisdiction, but they generally require certain professionals or individuals to report suspected or witnessed elder abuse to appropriate authorities. Mandatory reporters often include healthcare professionals, social workers, law enforcement personnel, and caregivers. Failure to report abuse can result in legal consequences, such as fines or penalties.

The legal obligations to report elder abuse serve several important purposes. They ensure that potential cases of abuse are brought to the attention of authorities, enabling timely intervention and protection of older adults. Reporting also supports the collection of accurate data on the prevalence of elder abuse, aiding in policy development and resource allocation to address this issue effectively.

Ethical Responsibilities of Professionals and Individuals

Beyond legal obligations, professionals and individuals involved in the care and support of older adults have ethical responsibilities to report elder abuse. Ethical considerations prioritize the well-being, dignity, and autonomy of the older adult. Reporting abuse aligns with ethical principles, such as beneficence (promoting the well-being of the older adult), non-maleficence (preventing harm), and justice (advocating for fairness and protection of vulnerable individuals).

Professionals, including healthcare providers, social workers, and caregivers, have ethical duties to act in the best interest of their clients or patients. They must recognize and respond promptly to signs of abuse, maintaining confidentiality and privacy while balancing the need to protect the older adult from harm. Reporting abuse allows professionals to fulfill their ethical responsibilities by ensuring that appropriate interventions are implemented to safeguard the well-being of older adults.

Challenges and Dilemmas

Reporting elder abuse can present challenges and dilemmas for professionals and individuals. Some common challenges include

1. Lack of Evidence: In some cases, there may be limited evidence or uncertainty about whether abuse is occurring. Professionals may be unsure whether the signs observed are indicative of abuse or a result of other factors. Balancing the

need to report with the potential harm that false allegations may cause requires careful consideration.

Confidentiality and Privacy

2. Professionals must navigate the delicate balance between respecting the older adult's confidentiality and privacy rights and the duty to protect them from harm. They should ensure that reporting is done in a manner that minimizes the risk of further harm or breach of confidentiality.

Cultural and Ethical Considerations

3. Different cultures may have distinct perspectives on elder abuse and reporting practices. Professionals must approach reporting in a culturally sensitive manner, taking into account the values, beliefs, and preferences of the older adult and their community.

Retaliation and Safety Concerns

4. Reporting abuse can potentially expose the older adult to retaliation or escalate the risk of harm. Professionals should assess the safety of the older adult and take appropriate measures to protect them during the reporting process.

Strategies to Enhance Reporting

To enhance reporting of elder abuse while addressing the challenges and dilemmas, several strategies can be implemented

5. Education and Training: Providing comprehensive education and training on recognizing the signs of elder abuse, the reporting process, and ethical considerations can empower professionals and individuals to respond appropriately and confidently.

Supportive Reporting Systems

6. Establishing supportive reporting systems that ensure confidentiality, protect the reporter's identity, and provide guidance and resources can encourage individuals to come forward and report abuse.

Collaboration and Communication

7. Encouraging collaboration and communication among professionals, agencies, and stakeholders involved in elder abuse prevention and intervention can improve the coordination of reporting efforts and ensure a holistic response to cases of abuse.

Ethical Decision-Making Frameworks

8. Developing ethical decision-making frameworks that consider the unique circumstances of each case can assist professionals in navigating the complexities and dilemmas associated with reporting elder abuse.

Multidisciplinary Approach

9. Adopting a multidisciplinary approach that involves professionals from different fields, such as healthcare, social services, and legal professions, can facilitate a comprehensive assessment of the situation and appropriate intervention measures.

Reporting elder abuse is both a legal obligation and an ethical responsibility. Professionals and individuals involved in the care and support of older adults must recognize the signs of abuse, understand the legal obligations to report, and navigate the potential challenges and dilemmas that may arise. By enhancing education, establishing supportive reporting systems, promoting collaboration and communication, and utilizing ethical decision-making frameworks, we can create an environment where reporting elder abuse is encouraged, facilitated, and appropriately addressed. By upholding the rights and well-being of older adults, we can work towards a society that protects and respects its most vulnerable members.

Approaches to Intervention and Support in Elder Abuse

Intervention and support are essential components in addressing elder abuse effectively and promoting the safety and well-being of older adults. In this chapter, we will explore various approaches to intervention and support for elder abuse victims. We will discuss the importance of a multidisciplinary approach, examine different intervention strategies, and explore the role of support services in helping older adults recover and thrive. By understanding and implementing these approaches, we can work towards creating a society that provides comprehensive support to those affected by elder abuse.

Multidisciplinary Approach to Intervention

1. Identification and Assessment: Professionals from various disciplines work together to identify cases of elder abuse and conduct comprehensive assessments to determine the extent of the abuse, the safety of the older adult, and their specific needs.

Communication and Information Sharing

2. Effective communication and information sharing among professionals are crucial for coordinated intervention efforts. Regular case conferences, sharing of relevant information, and

joint decision-making ensure a holistic approach to addressing elder abuse.

Collaboration and Referral

3. Professionals collaborate to provide appropriate referrals and connect older adults with the necessary support services. This may include medical care, counseling, legal aid, housing assistance, and financial support.

Advocacy and Legal Support

4. Legal professionals and advocates play a vital role in supporting elder abuse victims. They provide legal advice, assist with protective orders, navigate the legal system, and advocate for the rights and best interests of the older adult.

Intervention Strategies:Safety Planning

5. Safety planning involves developing personalized strategies to ensure the immediate safety of the older adult. This may include identifying safe spaces, establishing emergency contacts, and implementing protective measures to prevent further abuse.

Counseling and Emotional Support

6. Counseling services, including individual therapy, support groups, and trauma-informed care, help older adults address the emotional and psychological impact of abuse. These services provide a safe space for expression, healing, and developing coping strategies.

Medical Intervention

7. Healthcare professionals play a crucial role in addressing the physical consequences of abuse, conducting medical

examinations, treating injuries, and addressing the overall health needs of older adults. Medical intervention also includes assessing and managing the impact of abuse on mental health, including depression, anxiety, and post-traumatic stress disorder (PTSD).

Legal Intervention

8. Legal intervention involves taking appropriate legal actions to protect the older adult and hold perpetrators accountable. This may include seeking protective orders, pursuing criminal charges, or advocating for the older adult's rights in legal proceedings.

Advocacy and Empowerment

9. Advocacy aims to empower older adults by providing them with information about their rights, assisting in decision-making, and supporting their autonomy. Advocates work alongside older adults to help them navigate systems, access resources, and ensure their voices are heard.

Support Services

10. Case Management: Case managers play a crucial role in coordinating services and providing ongoing support to older adults. They assess needs, develop care plans, connect individuals with appropriate services, and monitor progress to ensure the provision of comprehensive support.

Financial Assistance

11. Financial assistance programs can help older adults recover from financial exploitation or abuse. These programs may include reimbursement for stolen assets, assistance with

housing or utility payments, or accessing benefits and entitlements.

Housing Support

12. Providing safe and suitable housing options is vital for older adults experiencing abuse. Support services may include transitional housing, emergency shelters, or assistance with relocating to safer environments.

Caregiver Support

13. Support services for caregivers play an important role in preventing abuse and promoting healthy caregiving relationships. These services may include respite care, training programs, counseling, and support groups.

Community Integration

14. Social connections and community engagement are crucial for older adults recovering from abuse. Community integration services focus on providing opportunities for socialization, participation in activities, and access to community resources.

Effective intervention and support are essential in addressing elder abuse and promoting the safety, well-being, and recovery of older adults. A multidisciplinary approach ensures a comprehensive response that addresses the complex factors contributing to elder abuse. Intervention strategies such as safety planning, counseling, medical and legal interventions, and advocacy empower older adults and hold perpetrators accountable. Support services, including case management, financial assistance, housing support, caregiver support, and community integration, provide the necessary resources for healing and rebuilding lives. By implementing these approaches, we can create a society that protects and supports older adults, ensuring their safety, dignity, and well-being in the face of elder abuse.

Chapter 6
Preventing Elder Abuse

Preventing elder abuse is crucial for promoting the safety, well-being, and dignity of older adults. In this chapter, we will explore various strategies and approaches to prevent elder abuse. We will discuss the importance of awareness and education, address risk factors and protective factors, examine community and policy-level interventions, and emphasize the role of individuals and society in preventing elder abuse. By understanding and implementing preventive measures, we can create a society that values and safeguards the rights of older adults.

Awareness and Education

Raising awareness and providing education about elder abuse is a fundamental step in prevention. This includes

Public Awareness Campaigns

1. Launching campaigns to increase public awareness about the signs, types, and consequences of elder abuse. These campaigns can be conducted through various mediums, such as television, radio, social media, and community events.

Professional Training

2. Providing training to professionals who interact with older adults, such as healthcare providers, social workers, law enforcement officers, and caregivers. Training programs

should focus on recognizing the signs of abuse, understanding risk factors, and promoting appropriate intervention strategies.

Community Education

3. Conducting educational workshops and seminars in communities to inform older adults, their families, and caregivers about elder abuse, prevention strategies, and available support services.

Risk Factors and Protective Factors

Understanding the risk factors and protective factors associated with elder abuse is crucial for prevention efforts. Risk factors increase the likelihood of abuse, while protective factors act as buffers against abuse. Some examples include:

Risk Factors

1. Social isolation and loneliness: Older adults who lack social connections and support networks are more vulnerable to abuse.

Caregiver stress

2. Caregivers experiencing high levels of stress, burnout, or lack of support are more likely to engage in abusive behaviors.

Cognitive impairment

Older adults with cognitive impairments, such as dementia, may be at higher risk due to their increased dependency on others.

History of family violence

1. A family history of violence increases the likelihood of elder abuse within that family.

Protective Factors

2. Social support: Having a strong social support system, including family, friends, and community, can reduce the risk of abuse by providing assistance and companionship.

Adequate caregiver support

3. Ensuring caregivers have access to support services, respite care, and training can alleviate stress and reduce the risk of abuse.

Access to healthcare

4. Regular healthcare visits and comprehensive medical care can promote early detection of abuse and provide interventions.

Financial security

5. Adequate financial resources and financial literacy can reduce the risk of financial exploitation.

Community and Policy-Level Interventions

6. Preventing elder abuse requires community and policy-level interventions. Some key strategies include

Establishing Supportive Communities

7. Creating age-friendly communities that promote social inclusion, access to services, and intergenerational connections can reduce social isolation and increase protective factors for older adults.

Strengthening Caregiver Support

8. Providing caregiver support programs, respite care services, and training opportunities can alleviate caregiver stress, enhance caregiving skills, and reduce the risk of abuse.

Promoting Collaboration and Information Sharing

9. Encouraging collaboration among professionals, agencies, and community organizations to share information, coordinate services, and develop a comprehensive response to elder abuse cases.

Legislative and Policy Changes

10. Implementing and enforcing laws and policies that protect the rights of older adults, address financial exploitation, and enhance reporting and intervention systems. This includes strengthening adult protective services, guardianship laws, and elder abuse reporting requirements.

Individual and Societal Responsibilities

Preventing elder abuse is a collective responsibility that involves both individuals and society. Key responsibilities include

Respecting Older Adults

1. Respecting the rights, autonomy, and dignity of older adults is essential in preventing abuse. This includes treating them with kindness, empathy, and respect, valuing their opinions and decisions, and ensuring their participation in decision-making processes.

Building Strong Support Networks

2. Building strong support networks within families, communities, and institutions to provide social support, companionship, and assistance to older adults. This can be achieved through community programs, volunteer initiatives, and intergenerational activities.

Reporting Suspected Abuse

3. Encouraging individuals to report suspected cases of elder abuse to the appropriate authorities or helplines. Creating a safe and confidential reporting environment is crucial to overcome barriers and ensure that abuse is addressed promptly.

Promoting Ageism Awareness

4. Addressing ageism and promoting positive attitudes towards aging can challenge stereotypes and reduce the risk of elder abuse. Society should value and celebrate the contributions of older adults and advocate for their rights.

Preventing elder abuse requires a multi-faceted approach that involves awareness and education, understanding risk and protective factors, implementing community and policy-level interventions, and recognizing individual and societal responsibilities. By increasing awareness, promoting education, addressing risk factors, enhancing protective factors, and implementing community and policy-level interventions, we can create a society that respects, protects, and supports older adults. Preventing elder abuse is not only a moral imperative but also a necessary step towards ensuring the well-being and dignity of older adults as they age.

Promoting Awareness and Education on Elder Abuse

Promoting awareness and education on elder abuse is a crucial step in preventing and addressing this pervasive issue. In this chapter, we will explore the significance of awareness and education, discuss the key stakeholders involved, examine effective strategies to promote awareness, and emphasize the importance of education in empowering individuals and communities to prevent elder abuse. By understanding and implementing these approaches, we can create a society that recognizes and actively addresses elder abuse.

The Significance of Awareness and Education

Awareness and education play a fundamental role in preventing elder abuse. They serve several purposes

Recognition of Elder Abuse

1. Many cases of elder abuse go unnoticed or unrecognized due to various factors, including lack of awareness. By promoting awareness, individuals can identify the signs and types of abuse, thereby increasing the chances of early detection and intervention.

Empowering Older Adults

2. Awareness and education empower older adults by informing them about their rights, helping them recognize abusive situations, and providing them with knowledge and resources to protect themselves. This empowerment allows older adults to take proactive measures to prevent abuse and seek help when needed.

Challenging Stereotypes and Stigma

3. Awareness efforts can challenge ageist stereotypes and reduce the stigma associated with elder abuse. By promoting a culture that respects and values older adults, we create an environment where abuse is less likely to occur and more likely to be reported.

Encouraging Reporting

4. Raising awareness about reporting mechanisms and creating a supportive environment encourages individuals to report

suspected cases of elder abuse. Increased reporting leads to timely intervention, protection for victims, and holding perpetrators accountable.

Stakeholders Involved in Promoting Awareness and Education

Promoting awareness and education on elder abuse requires collaboration among various stakeholders

Government and Non-Profit Organizations

5. Government agencies, such as departments of aging or social services, and non-profit organizations focused on elder rights and well-being, play a vital role in initiating awareness campaigns, providing educational resources, and coordinating prevention efforts.

Healthcare Professionals

6. Healthcare providers, including doctors, nurses, and social workers, are often in a prime position to identify and address elder abuse. They can incorporate elder abuse screenings into routine assessments, provide information and resources to patients, and promote awareness within their professional networks.

Community and Faith-Based Organizations

7. Community organizations, such as senior centers, faith-based groups, and social clubs, can facilitate awareness programs, workshops, and support groups within local communities. These organizations often have established relationships with older adults and can effectively disseminate information.

Law Enforcement and Legal Professionals

8. Law enforcement agencies and legal professionals are key stakeholders in promoting awareness and education on elder abuse. They can provide training to personnel, develop protocols for responding to abuse cases, and advocate for legal protections for older adults.

Strategies to Promote Awareness: Public Awareness Campaigns

Launching public awareness campaigns through various media channels, including television, radio, print, and social media platforms. These campaigns should highlight the signs, types, and consequences of elder abuse, as well as available support services and reporting mechanisms.

Educational Workshops and Seminars

1. Conducting educational workshops and seminars for older adults, their families, caregivers, and professionals in healthcare, social services, and law enforcement. These sessions can cover topics such as recognizing abuse, understanding rights and resources, and promoting prevention strategies.

Training Programs for Professionals

2. Providing specialized training programs for professionals who work with older adults, such as healthcare providers, social workers, and caregivers. These programs should focus on identifying and addressing elder abuse, cultural competency, ethical considerations, and intervention strategies.

Collaboration and Partnerships

3. Collaborating with various stakeholders, including government agencies, non-profit organizations, and community groups, to pool resources, share information, and develop comprehensive awareness campaigns. By working together, stakeholders can reach a wider audience and maximize the impact of their efforts.

Educational Materials and Resources

4. Developing and disseminating educational materials, such as brochures, pamphlets, posters, and online resources, that provide clear information on elder abuse, prevention strategies, and available support services. These materials should be accessible, culturally appropriate, and available in multiple languages.

The Importance of Education

Education plays a critical role in preventing elder abuse

Empowering Individuals

1. Education empowers individuals by providing them with knowledge about elder abuse, including its signs, risk factors, and prevention strategies. With this knowledge, individuals can recognize and respond to abusive situations effectively.

Fostering a Culture of Respect

2. Education promotes a culture of respect for older adults by challenging ageist stereotypes, promoting positive attitudes towards aging, and emphasizing the value and dignity of older individuals. This cultural shift reduces the likelihood of elder abuse and creates an environment where abuse is not tolerated.

Encouraging Ethical Decision-Making

3. Education on ethical considerations related to elder abuse equips individuals with the tools to make informed decisions and take appropriate actions when encountering potential abuse. It emphasizes the importance of upholding the rights and well-being of older adults.

Strengthening Support Networks

4. Education fosters stronger support networks by providing information about available resources, support services, and reporting mechanisms. Individuals become aware of where to seek help and how to support older adults who may be at risk.

Promoting awareness and education on elder abuse is a vital component of prevention efforts. By raising awareness, empowering individuals, challenging stereotypes, and fostering a culture of respect, we create an environment where elder abuse is less likely to occur and more likely to be reported. Collaboration among stakeholders, public awareness campaigns, educational workshops, and the dissemination of resources are key strategies to enhance awareness and education. Education empowers individuals, promotes ethical decision-making, and strengthens support networks. Through these efforts, we can build a society that recognizes and prevents elder abuse, ensuring the safety, well-being, and dignity of older adults.

Strengthening Support Networks and Resources in Elder Abuse Prevention

Strengthening support networks and resources is essential for preventing and addressing elder abuse effectively. In this chapter, we will explore the significance of support networks, discuss the key components of a robust support system, examine the role of community organizations and services, and emphasize the importance of accessible and comprehensive resources. By understanding and enhancing support networks and resources, we can create a supportive environment for older adults and effectively prevent elder abuse.

The Significance of Support Networks

Support networks provide a vital safety net for older adults and play a critical role in elder abuse prevention. They offer emotional support, assistance, and resources that can help older adults maintain their well-being, resilience, and independence. The significance of support networks includes:

Social Connection and Engagement

Support networks provide opportunities for social interaction, companionship, and engagement with peers, family members, and community organizations. Social connections reduce social isolation, which is a risk factor for elder abuse, and promote overall well-being.

Early Detection and Intervention

Support networks increase the likelihood of early detection and intervention in cases of elder abuse. Trusted individuals within the network may observe signs of abuse or changes in behavior, leading to prompt reporting and appropriate intervention to protect the older adult.

Information and Resource Sharing

Support networks offer a platform for sharing information, resources, and knowledge about elder abuse prevention, available services, and reporting mechanisms. This exchange of information equips network members with the tools to recognize and respond effectively to elder abuse.

Advocacy and Empowerment

Support networks advocate for the rights, dignity, and well-being of older adults. They empower older adults to assert their rights, make informed decisions, and seek assistance when needed. Advocacy within support networks helps challenge ageist attitudes and societal norms that perpetuate elder abuse.

Components of a Robust Support System

A robust support system comprises various components that work together to prevent elder abuse and support older adults

Community Organizations

Community organizations, such as senior centers, faith-based groups, and local nonprofits, provide a range of services and activities that foster social connection, offer educational programs, and promote the well-being of older adults. They serve as hubs for networking, support, and resource dissemination.

Helplines and Hotlines

Helplines and hotlines offer confidential and accessible support for older adults, caregivers, and concerned individuals. Trained professionals provide information, crisis intervention, emotional support, and guidance on reporting elder abuse.

Support Groups

Support groups bring together individuals who share similar experiences or challenges related to aging or caregiving. These groups provide a platform for mutual support, sharing of coping strategies, and empowerment. Support groups can be specialized, focusing on topics such as elder abuse prevention or caregiver support.

Care Coordination and Case Management

Care coordination and case management services help older adults navigate the complexities of accessing and coordinating healthcare, social services, and support systems. These services ensure that older adults receive appropriate and coordinated care, tailored to their specific needs.

Legal Aid and Advocacy Services

Legal aid services provide older adults with legal representation, advice, and assistance in navigating legal processes related to elder abuse. Advocacy services work to protect the rights and interests of older adults, ensuring their voices are heard and respected.

Accessible and Comprehensive Resources

Accessible and comprehensive resources are crucial in supporting older adults and preventing elder abuse

Informational Materials

Providing informational materials, such as brochures, fact sheets, and websites, that educate older adults, caregivers, and the general public about elder abuse, prevention strategies, available support services, and reporting mechanisms. These materials should be culturally sensitive, available in multiple languages, and easily accessible.

Training and Educational Programs

Developing training programs and workshops that educate professionals, caregivers, and community members about recognizing and responding to elder abuse. These programs should cover topics such as identifying abuse, ethical considerations, and intervention strategies.

Financial Assistance Programs

Offering financial assistance programs that can help older adults recover from financial exploitation or abuse. These programs may include reimbursement for stolen assets, assistance with legal fees, or financial counseling services.

Collaboration with Service Providers

Collaborating with healthcare providers, social services agencies, law enforcement, legal professionals, and other service providers to ensure a coordinated and integrated approach in supporting older adults. This collaboration ensures that older adults have access to comprehensive services that address their physical, emotional, and social needs.

Strengthening support networks and resources is vital for preventing elder abuse and promoting the well-being of older adults. Support networks provide social connection, early detection, information sharing, and advocacy. A robust support system comprises community organizations, helplines, support groups, care coordination, and legal aid services. Accessible and comprehensive resources, including informational materials, training programs, financial assistance, and collaboration with service providers, enhance the effectiveness of support networks. By strengthening support networks and providing accessible resources, we can create a society that supports and protects older adults, ensuring their safety, well-being, and dignity.

CHAPTER 7
Empowering Older Adults

Empowering older adults is a crucial aspect of preventing elder abuse and promoting their overall well-being and independence. In this chapter, we will explore the significance of empowerment, discuss key components of empowering older adults, examine strategies to enhance empowerment, and emphasize the role of individuals, communities, and society in fostering empowerment. By understanding and promoting empowerment, we can create an environment where older adults are respected, supported, and able to live with dignity.

The Significance of Empowerment

Empowerment involves enabling older adults to assert their rights, make informed decisions, and actively participate in their own care and the decisions that affect their lives. Empowering older adults is significant for several reasons:

Prevention of Elder Abuse

Empowered older adults are better equipped to recognize and resist abusive situations. They have the confidence, knowledge, and agency to assert their boundaries, seek assistance when needed, and prevent abuse from occurring.

Enhancing Well-being and Quality of Life

Empowerment contributes to the overall well-being and quality of life of older adults. It promotes self-esteem, self-efficacy, and a sense of control over one's own life, leading to improved mental health, physical well-being, and satisfaction with life.

Promoting Autonomy and Self-Determination

Empowerment respects the autonomy and self-determination of older adults. It recognizes their right to make decisions about their own lives, including healthcare choices, financial matters, and living arrangements.

Combating Ageism

Empowering older adults challenges ageist stereotypes and societal norms that perpetuate discrimination and marginalization. It promotes a culture that values and respects the contributions, experiences, and wisdom of older adults.

Key Components of Empowering Older Adults

Empowering older adults involves addressing several key components

Information and Education

Providing older adults with information about their rights, available resources, and support services is essential. Education on topics such as elder abuse prevention, financial literacy, healthcare options, and legal rights equips older adults with the knowledge they need to make informed decisions and take action when necessary.

Decision-Making Autonomy

Recognizing and respecting the autonomy of older adults in decision-making processes is crucial. Older adults should be actively involved in decisions related to their care, finances, living arrangements, and overall well-being. Their preferences, values, and goals should be considered and respected.

Skills and Capacity Building

Enhancing the skills and capacities of older adults empowers them to navigate challenges, access support services, and advocate for their rights. Skills building can include financial management, technology literacy, self-advocacy, and communication skills.

Social Connection and Support

Fostering social connections and support networks is vital for older adults' empowerment. Engaging in social activities, participating in community groups, and maintaining relationships with family and friends provide older adults with a sense of belonging, support, and opportunities for engagement.

Strategies to Enhance Empowerment

Promoting Education and Lifelong Learning: Encouraging lifelong learning initiatives, such as continuing education programs, community classes, and online courses, ensures that older adults have access to educational opportunities that support their personal growth and empowerment.

Encouraging Active Participation

Encouraging older adults to actively participate in decision-making processes related to their care, housing, finances, and community activities. This can be achieved by creating inclusive environments, providing opportunities for input, and valuing their perspectives and experiences.

Providing Accessible Information and Resources

5. Ensuring that information and resources are easily accessible, available in multiple formats and languages, and tailored to the diverse needs of older adults. This includes providing clear instructions, simplifying complex information, and utilizing user-friendly technologies.

Offering Support Services

1. Providing a range of support services, such as counseling, legal aid, financial assistance, and healthcare navigation, that cater to the unique needs of older adults. These services empower older adults to access the support they need and make informed decisions.

Collaboration and Partnership

2. Collaborating with community organizations, service providers, and older adults themselves to develop and implement empowerment programs. Engaging older adults as active partners in the planning and delivery of services ensures that their voices are heard, and their perspectives are incorporated.

The Role of Individuals, Communities, and Society

Individuals, communities, and society as a whole have a crucial role to play in empowering older adults

Individuals

1. Older adults themselves can take steps to empower themselves by seeking information, asserting their rights, engaging in self-advocacy, and actively participating in decision-making processes. They can also contribute to the

empowerment of others by sharing their experiences, mentoring, and supporting fellow older adults.

Communities

2. Communities can create inclusive environments that value and respect older adults. They can facilitate opportunities for social connection, provide accessible resources and services, and promote intergenerational activities that foster mutual respect and understanding.

Society

3. Society at large should challenge ageism and discriminatory practices that undermine the empowerment of older adults. This includes advocating for policy changes that protect the rights of older adults, promoting positive portrayals of aging in media and popular culture, and fostering intergenerational solidarity.

Empowering older adults is essential for preventing elder abuse, promoting well-being, and combating ageism. By addressing key components such as information and education, decision-making autonomy, skills building, and social connection, we can enhance the empowerment of older adults. Strategies to enhance empowerment include promoting education, encouraging active participation, providing accessible resources, offering support services, and fostering collaboration and partnership. Individuals, communities, and society as a whole have a vital role to play in empowering older adults and creating a society that values and respects their rights, experiences, and contributions.

Encouraging Self-Advocacy and Independence

Encouraging self-advocacy and independence among older adults is essential for promoting their empowerment, well-being, and protection against elder abuse. In this chapter, we will explore the significance of self-advocacy and independence, discuss the benefits of fostering these qualities in older adults, examine strategies to encourage self-advocacy and independence, and emphasize the role of individuals, communities, and society in supporting older adults in these endeavors. By understanding and promoting self-advocacy and independence, we can create an environment where older adults are empowered to make decisions, assert their rights, and live with dignity.

The Significance of Self-Advocacy and Independence

Self-advocacy refers to older adults' ability to express their needs, assert their rights, and make informed decisions about their lives. Independence, on the other hand, involves older adults having control over their daily activities, maintaining their autonomy, and making choices that align with their preferences and values. Encouraging self-advocacy and independence among older adults is significant for several reasons:

Empowerment

Self-advocacy and independence empower older adults by giving them a voice in decisions that affect their lives. It allows them to actively participate in their own care, express their preferences, and take control of their well-being.

Protection against Abuse

Older adults who can advocate for themselves and assert their rights are less vulnerable to abuse. They can recognize and resist abusive situations, seek assistance when needed, and prevent exploitation or neglect.

Improved Quality of Life

Encouraging self-advocacy and independence enhances older adults' quality of life by promoting a sense of autonomy, purpose, and self-worth. It allows them to maintain their dignity, engage in activities they enjoy, and live according to their own values and beliefs.

Active Engagement

Self-advocacy and independence encourage older adults to remain actively engaged in society. It promotes social connection, fosters intergenerational relationships, and contributes to the overall well-being of both the individual and the community.

Strategies to Encourage Self-Advocacy and Independence:Education and Information

Providing older adults with education and information about their rights, available resources, and support services is crucial for empowering them to advocate for themselves. Workshops, seminars, and informational materials can equip older adults with the knowledge they need to make informed decisions and assert their rights.

Skill-Building

Offering skill-building opportunities that enhance older adults' abilities to communicate effectively, negotiate, and assert their needs and preferences. Skill-building workshops can focus on effective communication techniques, problem-solving strategies, and decision-making skills.

Encouraging Decision-Making Autonomy

Recognizing and respecting the autonomy of older adults in decision-making processes related to their care, living arrangements, finances, and overall well-being. Providing support and guidance while allowing older adults to take the lead in decision-making promotes their self-confidence and independence.

Establishing Supportive Environments

Creating environments that support self-advocacy and independence by fostering a culture of respect, active listening, and inclusion. Healthcare providers, social service agencies, and community organizations can adopt person-centered approaches that prioritize older adults' choices and preferences.

Peer Support and Mentoring

Facilitating peer support groups and mentoring programs where older adults can share experiences, offer guidance, and support one another in their journey towards self-advocacy and independence. Peer support provides a sense of belonging, validation, and encouragement.

The Role of Individuals, Communities, and Society

Individuals, communities, and society play significant roles in encouraging self-advocacy and independence among older adults

Individuals

Older adults can take active steps to develop self-advocacy skills and assert their independence. They can seek information, ask questions, express their preferences, and participate in decision-making processes. Older adults can also serve as role models for others, inspiring them to advocate for themselves.

Communities

Communities can create supportive environments that encourage self-advocacy and independence among older adults. This can be achieved through educational programs, community initiatives, and policies that promote active aging, respect for individual choices, and intergenerational integration.

Society

Society at large should challenge ageist attitudes and discriminatory practices that undermine the self-advocacy and independence of older adults. This includes promoting age-friendly policies, addressing barriers to participation, and valuing the contributions and experiences of older adults.

Encouraging self-advocacy and independence among older adults is crucial for their empowerment, well-being, and protection against elder abuse. Self-advocacy enables older adults to assert their rights, make informed decisions, and actively participate in their own care. Independence allows older adults to maintain control over their lives, engage in activities they enjoy, and live according to their preferences and values. By providing education, skill-building opportunities, and supportive environments, we can encourage older adults to advocate for themselves and assert their independence. The active involvement of individuals, communities, and society is essential in fostering self-advocacy and independence, creating a society that respects and supports the rights and choices of older adults.

Enhancing Social Connections and Engagement Enhancing social connections and engagement among older adults is vital for promoting their well-being, preventing social isolation, and reducing the risk of elder abuse. In this chapter, we will explore the significance of social connections and engagement, discuss the benefits of fostering these aspects in older adults, examine strategies to enhance social connections and engagement, and emphasize the role of individuals, communities, and society in supporting older adults in this endeavor. By understanding and promoting social connections and engagement, we can create a society that values the social well-being of older adults.

The Significance of Social Connections and Engagement

Social connections and engagement play a pivotal role in the lives of older adults

Well-being and Mental Health

Social connections provide emotional support, a sense of belonging, and opportunities for social interaction, which contribute to overall well-being and positive mental health outcomes. Engaging in social activities and maintaining meaningful relationships can reduce the risk of depression, anxiety, and cognitive decline.

Prevention of Social Isolation

Social connections and engagement are powerful antidotes to social isolation. By fostering connections with family, friends, and community members, older adults are less likely to experience feelings of loneliness and isolation, which are risk factors for elder abuse.

Cognitive Stimulation

Social engagement can provide cognitive stimulation through conversations, discussions, and participation in group activities.

Regular social interactions can help maintain cognitive function, memory, and overall brain health in older adults.

Physical Health

Social connections and engagement have been linked to better physical health outcomes. Engaging in social activities can promote an active lifestyle, encourage regular exercise, and provide motivation for maintaining healthy habits.

Benefits of Fostering Social Connections and Engagement

Fostering social connections and engagement among older adults yields numerous benefits

Sense of Belonging

Social connections provide older adults with a sense of belonging to a community, fostering a feeling of connectedness and support. This can enhance their overall life satisfaction and self-esteem.

Emotional Support

Social connections offer emotional support during challenging times. Having a network of trusted individuals to turn to for advice, empathy, and companionship can help older adults navigate life transitions, cope with stress, and mitigate the impact of adverse events.

Opportunities for Learning and Growth

Social engagement provides opportunities for older adults to learn new skills, acquire knowledge, and engage in intellectual pursuits. Participation in community activities, classes, and interest groups can foster personal growth, promote lifelong learning, and enhance cognitive abilities.

Meaningful Relationships

Social connections can lead to the development of meaningful relationships and friendships. These relationships provide a sense of camaraderie, shared experiences, and mutual support, fostering a sense of purpose and fulfillment.

Strategies to Enhance Social Connections and Engagement

Community Programs and Activities: Creating and promoting community programs and activities tailored to older adults' interests and needs. This may include social clubs, recreational classes, arts and crafts groups, volunteering opportunities, and intergenerational programs.

Intergenerational Interaction

Encouraging intergenerational interaction and activities that promote connections between older adults and younger generations. This can be achieved through mentoring programs, shared learning experiences, or collaborative community projects.

Supportive Housing Options

Developing supportive housing options that facilitate social interaction among older adults. This may include communal living arrangements, shared common spaces, and organized social activities within residential communities.

Technology and Digital Connectivity

Promoting the use of technology and digital connectivity to facilitate social connections. Older adults can utilize social media platforms, video conferencing tools, and online communities to stay connected with family and friends, engage in virtual interest groups, and access informational resources.

Peer Support Groups

Facilitating peer support groups that focus on specific interests, life transitions, or common experiences. These groups provide opportunities for older adults to share insights, provide emotional support, and learn from one another.

The Role of Individuals, Communities, and Society

Individuals, communities, and society as a whole have important roles in enhancing social connections and engagement among older adults

Individuals

Older adults can take the initiative to participate in community activities, engage in social events, and cultivate new relationships. Actively reaching out to others, attending social gatherings, and maintaining communication with family and friends can foster social connections and engagement.

Communities

Communities can create inclusive and age-friendly environments that promote social connections and engagement. This includes organizing community events, providing accessible transportation options, and facilitating opportunities for intergenerational interaction.

Society

Society at large should value and prioritize social connections among older adults. This includes promoting awareness about the importance of social engagement, combating ageism, and implementing policies that support community-based programs and activities for older adults.

Enhancing social connections and engagement is vital for the well-being and social inclusion of older adults. Social connections provide emotional support, prevent social isolation, and contribute to cognitive and physical health. By fostering social connections and engagement, older adults can experience a sense of belonging, emotional well-being, and opportunities for growth. Strategies such as community programs, intergenerational interaction, technology utilization, and peer support groups can enhance social connections and engagement among older adults. It is the collective responsibility of individuals, communities, and society to value and support social connections, creating a society that recognizes and promotes the social well-being of older adults.

CHAPTER 8
Building a Safer Future

Building a safer future for older adults involves taking proactive measures to prevent elder abuse, create supportive environments, and ensure the well-being and dignity of older adults. In this chapter, we will explore the significance of building a safer future, discuss key components of creating a safe environment, examine strategies to prevent elder abuse, and emphasize the role of individuals, communities, and society in safeguarding older adults. By understanding and implementing these strategies, we can work towards a future where older adults are protected from abuse and can age with safety and security.

The Significance of Building a Safer Future

Building a safer future for older adults is crucial for several reasons

Protection against Abuse

Elder abuse is a serious issue that affects the well-being and rights of older adults. By building a safer future, we can create an environment where abuse is prevented, detected, and addressed effectively. This ensures the physical, emotional, and financial safety of older adults.

Promotion of Dignity and Well-being

A safer future prioritizes the dignity and well-being of older adults. It acknowledges their rights, respects their autonomy, and provides supportive environments where they can age with independence, respect, and quality of life.

Prevention of Social Isolation

Building a safer future involves creating communities that promote social connections, engagement, and inclusion. By addressing social isolation, we reduce the vulnerability of older adults to abuse and neglect, as social connections serve as protective factors.

Cultivation of Age-Friendly Environments

A safer future involves developing age-friendly environments that cater to the unique needs of older adults. This includes accessible infrastructure, appropriate housing options, and healthcare systems that support the physical and emotional well-being of older adults.

Key Components of Creating a Safe Environment

Creating a safe environment for older adults involves several key components

Awareness and Education

Raising awareness about elder abuse, its signs, and the importance of prevention. Educating individuals, families, caregivers, and professionals about their roles and responsibilities in protecting older adults is vital.

Supportive Policies and Legislation

Implementing policies and legislation that protect the rights of older adults, address elder abuse, and establish reporting mechanisms. These policies should focus on prevention, intervention, and holding perpetrators accountable.

Collaborative Efforts

Encouraging collaboration among individuals, community organizations, healthcare providers, social services, law enforcement, and legal professionals. By working together, stakeholders can share information, resources, and expertise to prevent elder abuse and support victims.

Training and Capacity Building

Providing training programs to professionals, caregivers, and volunteers on recognizing and responding to elder abuse. This includes enhancing skills in communication, documentation, and intervention strategies to ensure effective support for older adults.

Strategies to Prevent Elder Abuse

Public Awareness Campaigns: Conducting public awareness campaigns to educate the general public about elder abuse, its types, and the importance of reporting. These campaigns can be delivered through various mediums, including television, radio, social media, and community events.

Financial Literacy Programs

Offering financial literacy programs for older adults to empower them with knowledge and skills to make informed financial decisions, prevent financial exploitation, and protect their assets.

Caregiver Support and Training

Providing support and training programs for caregivers to equip them with the necessary skills, knowledge, and resources to provide quality care without resorting to abuse or neglect.

Regular Screening and Assessment

Implementing regular screening and assessment protocols within healthcare settings, social services, and community organizations to identify signs of abuse or neglect. Prompt detection allows for timely intervention and support for older adults.

The Role of Individuals, Communities, and Society

Building a safer future for older adults requires collective efforts

Individuals

Individuals can play a significant role by promoting respectful and inclusive attitudes towards older adults, fostering social connections, and speaking out against elder abuse. They can report suspected cases of abuse and support older adults in accessing appropriate resources.

Communities

Communities can create safe spaces for older adults through age-friendly initiatives, community engagement programs, and the development of support networks. They can also collaborate with local authorities and organizations to establish coordinated response systems.

Society

Society as a whole should prioritize the well-being and rights of older adults by advocating for policies that protect them, promoting age-friendly environments, and challenging ageism and discrimination. Societal support is essential for building a culture that values and respects older adults.

Building a safer future for older adults is a collective responsibility that requires the active participation of individuals, communities, and society. By creating supportive environments, raising awareness, implementing protective policies, and fostering collaboration, we can prevent elder abuse and ensure the safety, well-being, and dignity of older adults. Strategies such as public awareness campaigns, financial literacy programs, caregiver support, and regular screening contribute to the prevention of elder abuse. Together, we can work towards a future where older adults can age with safety, security, and the respect they deserve.

Policy Recommendations and Legislative Changes

Policy recommendations and legislative changes are crucial for building a safer future for older adults, preventing elder abuse, and ensuring their protection, well-being, and dignity. In this chapter, we will explore the significance of policy and legislative actions, discuss key areas that require attention, examine specific policy recommendations, and emphasize the role of individuals, communities, and governments in implementing these changes. By understanding and advocating for policy reform, we can create a comprehensive framework that safeguards the rights and safety of older adults.

The Significance of Policy and Legislative Changes

Policy and legislative changes are essential for several reasons

Protection and Prevention

Policies and legislation provide a legal framework to protect the rights of older adults and prevent abuse. They establish guidelines, standards, and enforcement mechanisms that deter abuse and hold perpetrators accountable.

Awareness and Education

Policies can support awareness campaigns and educational programs that inform the public, professionals, caregivers, and older adults themselves about the signs of elder abuse, prevention strategies, and available support services.

Coordination and Collaboration

Policies encourage collaboration among various stakeholders, including healthcare providers, social services, law enforcement, legal professionals, and community organizations. They promote coordinated efforts to prevent abuse, share information, and provide support to older adults.

Funding and Resources

Policies that allocate funding and resources to elder abuse prevention initiatives can support research, training programs, support services, and interventions. Adequate funding ensures the implementation and sustainability of effective prevention strategies.

Key Areas Requiring Attention

Legal Definitions and ScopeReviewing and updating legal definitions of elder abuse to encompass the various forms of abuse, including physical, emotional, financial, and neglect. Clarifying the scope of abuse helps in identifying and addressing different manifestations of elder abuse effectively.

Reporting Mechanisms

Establishing accessible, confidential, and user-friendly reporting mechanisms for elder abuse. This includes hotlines, helplines, online reporting systems, and clear procedures for reporting and follow-up. Encouraging mandatory reporting for professionals in relevant fields can enhance detection and intervention.

Training and Education

Promoting mandatory training and education for professionals, caregivers, and individuals working with older adults. Training should cover identifying abuse, ethical considerations, intervention strategies, and support services. Continuous education ensures that professionals are up to date with best practices.

Enhanced Legal Protections

Strengthening legal protections for older adults by establishing specific legislation that addresses elder abuse. This may include increasing penalties for offenders, providing legal aid for victims, and expanding civil remedies for financial exploitation.

Policy Recommendations:National Elder Abuse Prevention Act

Enacting a comprehensive national elder abuse prevention act that outlines specific goals, funding mechanisms, and coordination efforts among federal agencies. This act would provide a unified approach to elder abuse prevention, research, training, and support services.

Mandatory Reporting Laws

Implementing mandatory reporting laws that require professionals in healthcare, social services, finance, and legal sectors to report suspected cases of elder abuse. This ensures timely intervention and support for older adults at risk.

Supportive Housing Standards

Developing and implementing standards for supportive housing facilities that ensure the safety, well-being, and dignity of older adults. These standards should cover physical safety measures, staffing requirements, abuse prevention protocols, and resident rights protections.

Elder Financial Exploitation Laws

Strengthening laws related to elder financial exploitation to provide better protection for older adults. This includes enhancing penalties for offenders, facilitating the recovery of stolen assets, and increasing resources for law enforcement to investigate financial crimes against older adults.

The Role of Individuals, Communities, and Governments

Building a safer future through policy and legislative changes requires collaboration among individuals, communities, and governments:

Individuals

Individuals can advocate for policy changes by raising awareness, contacting lawmakers, and joining advocacy groups focused on elder abuse prevention. They can also support older adults in accessing resources, reporting abuse, and seeking legal remedies.

Communities

Communities can play an active role by organizing campaigns, forums, and community events that raise awareness about elder abuse and the need for policy reform. They can collaborate with local governments and organizations to address gaps in services and advocate for policy changes.

Governments

Governments have a crucial role in enacting and implementing policies that protect older adults from abuse. They should prioritize elder abuse prevention in their legislative agendas, allocate funding for prevention programs, and establish regulatory frameworks to ensure compliance with elder abuse prevention standards.

Policy recommendations and legislative changes are essential for building a safer future for older adults, preventing elder abuse, and ensuring their protection and well-being. By addressing key areas such as legal definitions, reporting mechanisms, training, and legal protections, we can create a comprehensive framework that safeguards the rights and safety of older adults. Implementing policy recommendations, such as a national elder abuse prevention act, mandatory reporting laws, supportive housing standards, and enhanced elder financial exploitation laws, requires collaboration among individuals, communities, and governments. Together, we can advocate for policy reform and work towards a future where older adults are safe, protected, and able to age with dignity and security.

Collaboration and Community Initiatives

Collaboration and community initiatives play a vital role in building a safer future for older adults, preventing elder abuse, and fostering a supportive environment. In this chapter, we will explore the significance of collaboration and community-based efforts, discuss the benefits of these initiatives, examine strategies for effective collaboration, and emphasize the role of individuals, organizations, and communities in creating a collective response to elder abuse. By understanding the power of collaboration and community initiatives, we can work towards a society that prioritizes the well-being and protection of older adults.

The Significance of Collaboration and Community Initiatives

Collaboration and community initiatives are crucial for several reasons

Multi-Sectoral Approach

Elder abuse prevention requires the involvement of multiple sectors, including healthcare, social services, law enforcement, legal professionals, community organizations, and older adults themselves. Collaboration allows for a comprehensive response that addresses the diverse needs and challenges associated with elder abuse.

Enhanced Knowledge Sharing

Collaboration encourages the exchange of knowledge, best practices, and expertise among professionals and organizations. This sharing of information leads to a deeper understanding of elder abuse dynamics, effective prevention strategies, and the identification of emerging trends.

Coordinated Services

Collaboration enables the coordination of services and resources, ensuring that older adults have access to comprehensive support. By working together, organizations can streamline processes, eliminate duplication, and ensure a seamless continuum of care for older adults at risk.

Amplified Advocacy

Collaboration strengthens the collective voice advocating for policy changes, increased funding, and improved services for older adults. By joining forces, organizations and community members can amplify their advocacy efforts and drive systemic changes to protect older adults from abuse.

Benefits of Collaboration and Community Initiatives: Comprehensive Approach

Collaboration allows for a comprehensive approach to elder abuse prevention. By bringing together diverse perspectives, skills, and resources, community initiatives can address various aspects of abuse, including awareness, education, intervention, and support.

Increased Awareness

Community initiatives raise awareness about elder abuse, its signs, and prevention strategies. Through public campaigns, educational workshops, and community events, collaboration ensures that information reaches a wider audience, including older adults, caregivers, professionals, and community members.

Localized Solutions

Community initiatives are often tailored to the unique needs of the local population. By collaborating at the community level, organizations can develop targeted interventions that address specific risk factors, cultural considerations, and community dynamics.

Empowerment

Collaboration fosters a sense of empowerment among older adults and their communities. By involving older adults in decision-making processes, community initiatives empower them to share their experiences, voice their concerns, and actively participate in prevention efforts.

Strategies for Effective Collaboration: Establishing Partnerships

Building strong partnerships between organizations, service providers, and community groups is essential for effective collaboration. These partnerships can be formalized through memoranda of understanding, shared protocols, and joint projects.

Regular Communication

Open and regular communication is key to successful collaboration. Establishing communication channels, holding regular meetings, and sharing updates and information ensure that all stakeholders are informed and involved in decision-making processes.

Shared Data and Information

Collaboration requires the sharing of data, research findings, and best practices. Establishing protocols for data sharing and ensuring confidentiality safeguards promote transparency, trust, and informed decision-making.

Capacity Building

Investing in capacity-building initiatives, such as training programs and workshops, enhances the skills and knowledge of professionals, caregivers, and community members involved in elder abuse prevention. Building capacity ensures that collaborators are equipped to respond effectively to the needs of older adults.

The Role of Individuals, Organizations, and Communities

Building a safer future through collaboration and community initiatives requires active engagement from individuals, organizations, and communities:

Individuals

Individuals can contribute to collaboration efforts by participating in community initiatives, attending educational programs, and advocating for elder abuse prevention. By volunteering, donating, or sharing their expertise, individuals play a crucial role in creating a collective response to elder abuse.

Organizations

Organizations, including healthcare providers, social service agencies, law enforcement, legal professionals, and community groups, can collaborate by sharing resources, expertise, and networks. By working together, organizations can provide holistic support and services to older adults at risk.

Communities

Communities are the foundation of collaborative efforts. Engaged and supportive communities can raise awareness, mobilize resources, and foster a culture that values and protects older adults. Communities can facilitate the creation of elder-friendly environments and support initiatives that prevent elder abuse.

Collaboration and community initiatives are powerful tools in building a safer future for older adults and preventing elder abuse. By fostering multi-sectoral partnerships, sharing knowledge, and implementing localized solutions, community initiatives address the complex challenges associated with elder abuse. Collaboration enhances awareness, amplifies advocacy, and promotes a comprehensive approach to elder abuse prevention. The involvement of individuals, organizations, and communities is crucial in creating a collective response that ensures the well-being, protection, and dignity of older adults. Together, we can work towards a society that values and safeguards the rights of older adults, creating a safer and more inclusive future for all.

CHAPTER 9

Healing and Recovery

Healing and recovery are essential components of addressing elder abuse and promoting the well-being of older adults who have experienced abuse or neglect. In this chapter, we will explore the significance of healing and recovery, discuss the impacts of elder abuse on older adults' mental, emotional, and physical health, examine strategies and interventions for healing and recovery, and emphasize the importance of support systems and resources. By understanding the healing process and implementing effective interventions, we can contribute to the restoration and empowerment of older adults who have experienced abuse.

The Significance of Healing and Recovery: Healing and recovery are crucial for several reasons

Restoration of Dignity and Well-being: Healing and recovery processes aim to restore the dignity, autonomy, and well-being of older adults who have experienced abuse. It allows them to reclaim their sense of self-worth, regain control over their lives, and rebuild their confidence and trust in others.

Psychological and Emotional Well-being

Elder abuse can have profound psychological and emotional impacts on older adults, including feelings of shame, guilt, fear, anxiety, depression, and post-traumatic stress. Healing and recovery processes help address these emotional wounds, promoting mental well-being and overall quality of life.

Physical Health Improvement

Older adults who have experienced abuse may suffer physical injuries and have compromised health due to neglect or mistreatment. Healing and recovery processes focus on restoring physical health, providing necessary medical care, and supporting rehabilitation to improve their overall health outcomes.

Breaking the Cycle of Abuse

Healing and recovery not only benefit individual survivors but also contribute to breaking the cycle of abuse. By addressing the impacts of abuse and providing support, older adults are less likely to become victims or perpetrators of abuse in the future.

Impacts of Elder Abuse on Healing and Recovery

Elder abuse can have a significant impact on older adults' healing and recovery processes

Trust and Relationship Issues

Older adults who have experienced abuse may struggle with trust issues, making it challenging to form new relationships or seek help. Rebuilding trust and establishing supportive relationships is crucial for their healing journey.

Emotional Trauma

Elder abuse often leads to emotional trauma, affecting survivors' mental and emotional well-being. It is important to address and process these traumas through therapeutic interventions, counseling, and support groups.

Physical Rehabilitation

Healing and recovery may involve physical rehabilitation for older adults who have experienced physical abuse or neglect. This can include medical treatments, therapy, and assistance in regaining physical independence and mobility.

Strategies and Interventions for Healing and Recovery: Trauma-Informed Care

Adopting a trauma-informed approach in providing care and support to older adults who have experienced abuse. This approach acknowledges the impact of trauma and fosters an environment of safety, trust, and empowerment.

Counseling and Therapy

Providing individual or group counseling sessions to survivors of elder abuse. Therapeutic interventions can help survivors process their experiences, manage emotions, and develop coping strategies.

Support Groups

Facilitating support groups where survivors can connect with others who have experienced similar abuse. Support groups offer a sense of community, validation, and mutual support, reducing feelings of isolation and providing a platform for sharing experiences.

Rehabilitation Services

Collaborating with healthcare professionals and rehabilitation specialists to provide physical rehabilitation services. This may include physiotherapy, occupational therapy, and other specialized interventions to support physical healing and regain functional abilities.

Legal Support

Ensuring survivors have access to legal resources and support to seek justice and hold perpetrators accountable. Legal assistance can empower survivors and contribute to their healing process.

Importance of Support Systems and Resources

Creating a supportive environment and providing adequate resources is crucial for the healing and recovery of older adults who have experienced abuse

Supportive Networks

Encouraging the involvement of family, friends, and community members in supporting survivors' healing journeys. Social connections and a strong support network can provide emotional support, companionship, and practical assistance.

Community Services

Collaborating with community organizations, elder abuse prevention agencies, and social service providers to ensure survivors have access to a range of services, such as case management, housing support, transportation, and financial assistance.

Accessible Information

Ensuring that survivors have access to clear, accessible information about available resources, support services, and their rights. This includes providing information in multiple languages and formats to cater to diverse needs.

Continued Support

Recognizing that healing and recovery take time and providing ongoing support to survivors. This can include regular check-ins, follow-up services, and referrals to appropriate professionals or support groups.

Healing and recovery are integral components of addressing elder abuse and supporting older adults who have experienced mistreatment. By focusing on restoring dignity, promoting mental and physical well-being, and breaking the cycle of abuse, we can contribute to the healing and empowerment of survivors. Trauma-informed care, counseling, support groups, rehabilitation services, and legal support are key strategies and interventions that facilitate healing and recovery. Support systems and accessible resources play a crucial role in providing survivors with the necessary assistance, empowerment, and opportunities for rebuilding their lives. By prioritizing healing and recovery, we can create a society that values the well-being and rights of older adults, ensuring they can age with dignity and security.

Trauma-Informed Care for Elder Abuse Survivors

Trauma-informed care is a crucial approach in providing support and assistance to elder abuse survivors. It recognizes the impact of trauma on individuals' well-being, behaviors, and interactions, and aims to create a safe, empowering, and healing environment for survivors. In the context of elder abuse, trauma-informed care is essential in addressing the unique needs of older adults who have experienced mistreatment. In this chapter, we will explore the significance of trauma-informed care, discuss its key principles, examine its application in the context of elder abuse, and emphasize the role of professionals and organizations in implementing this approach. By understanding and implementing trauma-informed care, we can contribute to the healing and well-being of elder abuse survivors.

The Significance of Trauma-Informed Care

Trauma-informed care is significant for several reasons

Recognition of the Impact of Trauma

Elder abuse survivors may have experienced various forms of trauma, including physical, emotional, and financial abuse. Trauma-informed care acknowledges the impact of these traumatic experiences on survivors' overall well-being, mental health, and relationships.

Safety and Trust

Trauma-informed care prioritizes creating a safe and supportive environment for survivors. It promotes a sense of physical and emotional safety, allowing survivors to feel secure and comfortable in seeking help and support.

Empowerment and Collaboration

This approach empowers survivors by involving them in the decision-making process, respecting their autonomy, and valuing their experiences and perspectives. Collaboration between survivors and service providers fosters a sense of control, empowerment, and ownership of the healing process.

Avoidance of Re-traumatization

Trauma-informed care aims to prevent re-traumatization by understanding and minimizing triggers, providing choices, and utilizing techniques that promote emotional regulation and self-care.

Key Principles of Trauma-Informed Care: Safety

Creating a physically and emotionally safe environment for survivors by ensuring privacy, respect for boundaries, and open communication. Establishing trust is essential for survivors to feel safe in disclosing their experiences and seeking support.

Trustworthiness and Transparency

Building trust by providing clear information, maintaining consistent and honest communication, and following through on commitments. Transparency helps survivors feel secure and increases their confidence in the support they receive.

Choice and Control

Allowing survivors to make informed choices about their care and involving them in decision-making processes. Recognizing and respecting survivors' autonomy promotes their sense of control and empowerment.

Collaboration and Mutual Respect

Engaging in collaborative relationships with survivors, valuing their experiences, and incorporating their input into the care process. Mutual respect promotes a sense of equality and dignity for survivors.

Empowerment and Skill Building

Supporting survivors in developing skills and resources to cope with trauma and move towards healing. This may include providing information, teaching coping strategies, and connecting survivors with appropriate support services.

Application of Trauma-Informed Care in the Context of Elder Abuse

Sensitivity to Triggers

Trauma-informed care recognizes that certain triggers can evoke emotional and physiological responses in survivors. Service providers should be trained to identify and respond sensitively to these triggers, using strategies to minimize re-traumatization.

Emotional Safety

Creating an emotionally safe space for survivors to express their feelings and experiences without fear of judgment or dismissal. Active listening, empathy, and validation are essential in supporting survivors through the healing process.

Understanding the Complexity of Trauma

Recognizing that elder abuse survivors may have experienced multiple forms of trauma and that each individual's experience is unique. Taking a holistic approach allows for comprehensive care that addresses the specific needs and challenges of each survivor.

Collaboration and Supportive Relationships

Building collaborative relationships with survivors based on trust, empathy, and respect. Service providers should ensure that survivors have access to a multidisciplinary team of professionals who can offer comprehensive support.

Role of Professionals and Organizations: Training and Education

Professionals working with elder abuse survivors should receive training on trauma-informed care, recognizing the signs of trauma, and understanding the unique needs of older adults. Ongoing education ensures that professionals are equipped to provide appropriate support.

Creating Trauma-Informed Systems

Organizations should adopt trauma-informed practices at all levels, including policies, procedures, and organizational culture. This involves incorporating trauma-informed principles into service delivery, staff training, and continuous quality improvement.

Collaboration and Partnerships

Professionals and organizations should collaborate with other service providers, such as healthcare professionals, social workers, legal professionals, and community organizations. This collaboration ensures a coordinated and comprehensive response to the needs of elder abuse survivors.

Access to Resources

Organizations should ensure that survivors have access to a range of resources, such as counseling, support groups, legal assistance, and community services. Connecting survivors with appropriate resources helps facilitate their healing and recovery.

Trauma-informed care is a vital approach in supporting elder abuse survivors on their healing journey. By recognizing the impact of trauma, creating safe environments, fostering trust, and promoting empowerment, trauma-informed care enhances the well-being and resilience of survivors. Applying trauma-informed principles in the context of elder abuse requires sensitivity, collaboration, and ongoing training for professionals and organizations. By implementing trauma-informed care, we can contribute to the healing and empowerment of elder abuse survivors, ensuring they receive the support and care they need to move forward on their path to recovery.

Therapeutic Approaches and Support Services for Elder Abuse Survivors

Therapeutic approaches and support services are crucial in helping elder abuse survivors on their path to healing and recovery. These services aim to address the physical, emotional, and psychological impacts of abuse, provide a safe space for survivors to process their experiences, and empower them to regain control over their lives. In this chapter, we will explore the significance of therapeutic approaches and support services for elder abuse survivors, discuss different types of interventions, examine their benefits, and emphasize the importance of comprehensive and accessible support systems. By understanding and implementing these approaches, we can contribute to the well-being and resilience of elder abuse survivors.

The Significance of Therapeutic Approaches and Support Services: Emotional Healing

Elder abuse can result in profound emotional trauma for survivors. Therapeutic interventions provide a safe and supportive space for survivors to express their emotions, process their experiences, and work towards emotional healing and well-being.

Empowerment and Restoration of Control

Support services empower survivors by providing them with resources, information, and skills to regain control over their lives. These services help survivors recognize their strengths, build resilience, and develop strategies for moving forward.

Validation and Validation

Therapeutic approaches and support services validate survivors' experiences, providing a sense of validation, and acknowledging the harm they have endured. This validation can be crucial in the healing process, as it helps survivors rebuild their self-esteem and regain a sense of self-worth.

Access to Resources

Support services connect survivors with resources such as counseling, support groups, legal assistance, and medical care. These resources are essential in addressing survivors' unique needs and providing comprehensive support.

Types of Therapeutic Approaches and Support Services

Counseling and Therapy: Individual counseling and therapy provide a safe and confidential space for survivors to explore their experiences, express their emotions, and develop coping strategies. Therapists use evidence-based approaches such as cognitive-behavioral therapy (CBT), trauma-focused therapy, and person-centered therapy to support survivors in their healing journey.

Support Groups

Support groups bring together survivors who have experienced similar abuse, providing a sense of community, understanding, and validation. Support groups offer a platform for survivors to share their experiences, gain insights from others, and learn coping strategies from peers who have faced similar challenges.

Art Therapy

Art therapy utilizes creative processes such as painting, drawing, and writing to help survivors express their emotions, process their trauma, and foster self-discovery. Art therapy provides a non-verbal outlet for survivors to communicate their experiences and can be particularly beneficial for those who find it difficult to express themselves verbally.

Mindfulness and Meditation

Mindfulness and meditation practices help survivors develop self-awareness, manage stress, and cultivate a sense of calm. These practices focus on the present moment and help survivors build resilience, reduce anxiety, and enhance their overall well-being.

Trauma-Informed Yoga

Trauma-informed yoga incorporates gentle movement, breathing exercises, and mindfulness techniques to support survivors in reconnecting with their bodies, reducing physical tension, and promoting a sense of grounding. This approach emphasizes safety, choice, and empowerment during yoga practice.

Benefits of Therapeutic Approaches and Support Services

Emotional Healing and Well-being

Therapeutic approaches and support services provide survivors with tools and resources to process their trauma, manage their emotions, and enhance their overall well-being. These interventions empower survivors to develop healthy coping mechanisms and build resilience.

Validation and Empowerment

By providing survivors with a safe space to share their experiences, therapeutic approaches and support services validate their feelings and help rebuild their sense of self-worth. Survivors are empowered to take control of their lives, make informed choices, and set boundaries.

Social Support and Connection

Support services, such as support groups, foster a sense of community and connection among survivors. This social support network reduces feelings of isolation and provides a platform for sharing experiences, gaining insights, and building relationships with others who have faced similar challenges.

Education and Resources

Therapeutic approaches and support services provide survivors with information, education, and access to resources. This empowers survivors to make informed decisions about their future, understand their legal rights, access healthcare services, and navigate the support systems available to them.

Comprehensive and Accessible Support Systems

To ensure the effectiveness of therapeutic approaches and support services, it is essential to have comprehensive and accessible support systems in place

Integrated Services

Collaborative efforts between healthcare providers, social services, legal professionals, and community organizations are crucial in providing comprehensive support to survivors. Integrated services ensure that survivors can access multiple forms of support within a coordinated and holistic framework.

Culturally Competent Care

Support services should be culturally sensitive and consider the unique needs and experiences of diverse populations. Culturally competent care ensures that survivors from different backgrounds can access services that respect their cultural values, beliefs, and traditions.

Outreach and Awareness

Proactive outreach efforts are necessary to reach elder abuse survivors who may be unaware of the available support services. Raising awareness about elder abuse and the resources available for survivors can encourage help-seeking behaviors and increase access to support.

Adequate Funding and Resources

Governments, organizations, and community stakeholders should allocate sufficient funding and resources to support services for elder abuse survivors. Adequate funding enables the provision of quality services, training for professionals, and the development of innovative approaches to support survivors.

Therapeutic approaches and support services are vital in promoting the healing and well-being of elder abuse survivors. By addressing the emotional and psychological impacts of abuse, providing validation, empowering survivors, and connecting them with comprehensive support systems, we can help survivors on their journey towards healing and recovery. Counseling, support groups, art therapy, mindfulness practices, and trauma-informed yoga are just a few examples of the interventions that can support survivors in their healing process. It is crucial to ensure that these services are comprehensive, culturally competent, and easily accessible to survivors. By implementing and advocating for these services, we can contribute to the well-being and resilience of elder abuse survivors, ensuring they receive the support and care they deserve.

CHAPTER 10
Global Perspectives on Elder Abuse

Elder abuse is a pervasive issue that affects older adults worldwide, transcending geographic, cultural, and socioeconomic boundaries. In this chapter, we will explore global perspectives on elder abuse, discussing its prevalence, forms, and contributing factors in different regions. We will examine the challenges faced by various countries in addressing elder abuse and highlight international efforts, initiatives, and best practices in preventing and responding to this issue. By understanding global perspectives on elder abuse, we can foster awareness, advocate for change, and work towards a world where older adults are protected, respected, and valued.

Prevalence and Forms of Elder Abuse

Elder abuse occurs in various forms and is prevalent across different countries and regions

Physical Abuse

This involves the use of physical force that results in pain, injury, or impairment. It includes acts such as hitting, slapping, pushing, or restraining older adults.

Emotional and Psychological Abuse

Emotional abuse encompasses behaviors that cause emotional pain, distress, or fear. This can include insults, threats, intimidation, humiliation, or isolating older adults from social connections.

Financial Abuse

Financial abuse involves the misuse or exploitation of an older adult's financial resources. It can include theft, fraud, undue influence, or coercing older adults into signing documents against their will.

Neglect

Neglect occurs when a caregiver fails to meet the basic needs of an older adult, such as providing adequate food, shelter, medical care, or necessary support.

Sexual Abuse

Sexual abuse refers to non-consensual sexual contact, coercion, or exploitation of an older adult. It can involve unwanted sexual advances, assault, or forcing older adults to engage in sexual activities against their will.

Global Challenges in Addressing Elder Abuse

Addressing elder abuse poses several challenges at a global level

Underreporting

Elder abuse is often underreported due to factors such as fear, dependency on perpetrators, lack of awareness, cognitive impairments, or social stigma. This makes it difficult to assess the true extent of the problem and provide appropriate interventions.

Ageism and Cultural Norms

Ageism and cultural norms can perpetuate a lack of respect, value, and protection for older adults. Negative stereotypes and attitudes towards aging can contribute to the prevalence of elder abuse and hinder efforts to address the issue effectively.

Limited Resources and Capacity

Many countries face resource constraints in terms of funding, infrastructure, and trained professionals to address elder abuse. Limited capacity can impede the implementation of comprehensive prevention and response strategies.

International Efforts and Best Practices

Despite these challenges, international efforts are underway to address elder abuse

United Nations

The United Nations has recognized the importance of preventing and addressing elder abuse. The UN General Assembly designated June 15th as World Elder Abuse Awareness Day, raising global awareness and promoting actions to combat elder abuse.

World Health Organization (WHO)

The WHO provides guidance and resources on elder abuse prevention, including research, policy development, and training programs. The WHO's Global Status Report on Violence Prevention highlights elder abuse as a public health issue.

Legislation and Policies

Countries have enacted legislation and developed policies to protect older adults from abuse. These include laws that criminalize elder abuse, establish reporting mechanisms, and promote the rights and well-being of older adults.

Multidisciplinary Collaboration

Many countries have established multidisciplinary teams and task forces that bring together professionals from various sectors, including healthcare, social services, law enforcement, and legal professionals. This collaboration enhances prevention, identification, and response to elder abuse cases.

Awareness and Education

Public awareness campaigns and educational initiatives raise awareness about elder abuse, its signs, and available support services. These efforts aim to empower individuals, professionals, and communities to recognize, report, and prevent elder abuse.

Global perspectives on elder abuse highlight the need for collective action and international collaboration to protect and support older adults. By recognizing the prevalence and forms of elder abuse, understanding the challenges faced by different countries, and learning from international efforts and best practices, we can work towards effective prevention, intervention, and support systems. It is essential to promote awareness, challenge ageism, and advocate for policies that prioritize the rights, well-being, and dignity of older adults. Through concerted efforts, we can create a global society that values and protects older adults, ensuring their safety, respect, and inclusion in all corners of the world.

Cross-cultural Perspectives and Challenges in Addressing Elder Abuse

Elder abuse is a complex issue that manifests differently across cultures and societies. Understanding cross-cultural perspectives on elder abuse is essential to develop effective prevention and intervention strategies that respect diverse cultural norms, values, and practices. In this chapter, we will explore the cross-cultural perspectives on elder abuse, examine the challenges faced in addressing this issue across different cultures, and highlight the importance of culturally sensitive approaches. By acknowledging and respecting diverse cultural perspectives, we can work towards a global response that ensures the protection and well-being of older adults in all cultural contexts.

Cross-cultural Perspectives on Elder Abuse

Elder abuse is influenced by cultural, social, and economic factors that vary across different cultures and societies. Here are some key cross-cultural perspectives on elder abuse:

Cultural Norms and Values

Cultural norms and values shape attitudes towards aging, family dynamics, and the roles and responsibilities of older adults. In some cultures, traditional beliefs and practices may influence the perception of elder abuse or perpetuate ageism, making it more challenging to address the issue effectively.

Family Structures and Dynamics

Family structures play a significant role in elder abuse. In cultures with a strong emphasis on filial piety or intergenerational cohabitation, abuse may occur within family units due to caregiving stress, intergenerational conflicts, or power imbalances.

Social Support Networks

The availability and strength of social support networks vary across cultures. In collectivist cultures, where the family and community play a central role, elder abuse may be more hidden or underreported due to a sense of shame, stigma, or a desire to maintain family harmony.

Gender Dynamics

Gender norms and roles can influence the occurrence and perception of elder abuse. In cultures where gender inequality exists, older women may be particularly vulnerable to abuse, including financial exploitation and neglect.

1. Challenges in Addressing Elder Abuse Cross-culturally
2. Addressing elder abuse cross-culturally presents several challenges

Cultural Sensitivity

Developing effective strategies requires cultural sensitivity and an understanding of diverse cultural contexts. Approaches to prevention, intervention, and support must respect cultural values, beliefs, and practices to ensure acceptance and engagement from affected communities.

Language and Communication Barriers

Language barriers may hinder effective communication and reporting of elder abuse. Culturally appropriate translation services and interpreters can bridge this gap and ensure that older adults can express their experiences and seek assistance.

Underreporting and Shame

Cultural norms and stigma surrounding elder abuse may contribute to underreporting. Older adults may feel ashamed or fear repercussions, making it difficult to obtain accurate data and provide appropriate support.

Legal and Policy Challenges

Legal and policy frameworks addressing elder abuse may differ across cultures. Developing comprehensive and culturally sensitive legislation that protects older adults' rights while respecting cultural values is crucial but challenging.

Culturally Sensitive Approaches

To overcome these challenges, culturally sensitive approaches must be implemented

Community Engagement and Collaboration

Engaging with community leaders, elders, and local organizations fosters trust and ensures that interventions are culturally appropriate and acceptable. Collaboration with community stakeholders is essential in designing prevention programs, raising awareness, and providing support services.

Culturally Tailored Education and Awareness

Culturally tailored education programs raise awareness about elder abuse, its signs, and available resources. Materials and outreach efforts should be sensitive to cultural nuances, languages, and literacy levels.

Culturally Competent Service Providers

Training professionals to understand and respect diverse cultural perspectives is essential. Service providers should receive education on cultural norms, values, and practices to ensure culturally competent and respectful interactions with older adults.

Empowering Community Leaders

Engaging community leaders and organizations empowers them to take a lead in addressing elder abuse within their cultural context. Empowering these leaders can facilitate the dissemination of information, promote positive cultural change, and reduce stigma.

Cross-cultural perspectives on elder abuse highlight the importance of understanding and respecting diverse cultural contexts when addressing this issue. Culturally sensitive approaches that consider cultural norms, values, and practices are crucial in developing effective prevention and intervention strategies. Collaboration with community leaders, tailored education programs, culturally competent service providers, and empowering community members are essential components of a comprehensive response to elder abuse. By embracing cross-cultural perspectives, we can ensure the protection and well-being of older adults in all cultural contexts and work towards a world where elder abuse is prevented and older adults are respected and valued.

Creating a World Free from Elder Abuse

Elder abuse is a significant global issue that demands collective efforts to create a world where older adults are protected, respected, and valued. Throughout this book, we have explored various aspects of elder abuse, including its definitions, types, impacts, factors contributing to it, interventions, and global perspectives. Now, in the concluding chapter, we will emphasize the importance of creating a world free from elder abuse, discuss key strategies to achieve this goal, and highlight the role of individuals, communities, organizations, and policymakers in making it a reality. By working together, we can ensure the well-being, safety, and dignity of older adults and foster a society that cherishes and protects its elder population.

The Importance of Creating a World Free from Elder Abuse

Creating a world free from elder abuse is essential for several reasons

Human Rights and Dignity

Every individual, regardless of age, deserves to be treated with respect, dignity, and compassion. Elder abuse infringes upon the fundamental human rights of older adults and undermines their inherent worth and value.

Well-being and Quality of Life

Elder abuse has severe physical, emotional, and psychological impacts on older adults. By preventing and addressing elder abuse, we can contribute to their overall well-being, promoting healthier and more fulfilling lives for older adults.

Inter-generational Harmony

A world free from elder abuse fosters inter-generational harmony and strengthens family and community bonds. By promoting positive relationships, respect, and support between generations, we build a society that values the wisdom and contributions of older adults.

Strategies for Creating a World Free from Elder Abuse: Awareness and Education

Raising awareness about elder abuse is critical in changing societal attitudes, dispelling myths, and encouraging early intervention. Educational initiatives should target individuals of all ages, professionals, communities, and policymakers to promote understanding and proactive responses to elder abuse.

Prevention

Prioritizing prevention efforts is essential in reducing the occurrence of elder abuse. This involves addressing the root causes of abuse, such as ageism, social isolation, caregiver stress, and financial exploitation. Prevention strategies may include community outreach, caregiver support programs, financial literacy initiatives, and social connection programs for older adults.

Support Services

Accessible and comprehensive support services are crucial in addressing elder abuse. This includes providing counseling, legal assistance, healthcare support, and social services tailored to the specific needs of older adults. Collaboration between healthcare professionals, social workers, legal experts, and community organizations can ensure the availability of diverse and holistic support systems.

Policy and Legislation

Governments and policymakers play a vital role in creating an environment that protects older adults from abuse. Strengthening legal frameworks, developing robust elder abuse legislation, and implementing policies that promote the rights and well-being of older adults are crucial steps in combating elder abuse.

Multidisciplinary Collaboration

Combating elder abuse requires a multidisciplinary approach involving various sectors and stakeholders. Collaboration between healthcare providers, social service agencies, legal professionals, law enforcement, community groups, and researchers enables the pooling of resources, expertise, and knowledge to create a comprehensive and coordinated response to elder abuse.

The Role of Individuals, Communities, Organizations, and Policymakers: Individuals

Each individual can contribute to a world free from elder abuse by respecting and valuing older adults, supporting older family members and neighbors, advocating for elder rights, and reporting any signs of abuse or neglect. By fostering inter-generational connections, promoting empathy, and challenging ageism, individuals can play a vital role in preventing elder abuse.

Communities

Communities have the power to create an environment that protects older adults. By fostering a culture of respect, inter-generational collaboration, and social inclusion, communities can reduce social isolation, promote well-being, and create support networks that prevent elder abuse.

Organizations

Organizations, including nonprofits, advocacy groups, and service providers, have a responsibility to prioritize elder abuse prevention and support. By providing resources, education, support services, and collaborative platforms, organizations can contribute to creating a world where elder abuse is not tolerated.

Policymakers

Policymakers have the authority to enact legislation and develop policies that protect the rights and well-being of older adults. By prioritizing elder abuse prevention, funding support services, and incorporating elder rights into national agendas, policymakers can create an environment that fosters respect, safety, and dignity for older adults.

Conclusion

This book has explored the multifaceted issue of elder abuse, providing a comprehensive understanding of its various aspects, impacts, and strategies for addressing and preventing it. Elder abuse is a global concern that transcends geographical, cultural, and socioeconomic boundaries, affecting the lives of older adults in diverse ways. Throughout the chapters, we have delved into the definition of elder abuse, its different forms such as physical, emotional, financial, and neglect, and the complex factors contributing to its occurrence.

One of the key takeaways from this book is the recognition of the profound impact that elder abuse has on older adults. It affects their physical health, emotional well-being, and overall quality of life. Elder abuse strips older adults of their dignity, autonomy, and sense of security, undermining their fundamental human rights. By understanding the far-reaching consequences of elder abuse, we can better appreciate the urgency and importance of addressing this issue.

Moreover, this book has emphasized the significance of prevention and early intervention in combating elder abuse. By raising awareness, promoting education, and fostering a culture of respect and support for older adults, we can create an environment that is less conducive to abuse. Prevention strategies should target not only individuals but also communities, organizations, and policymakers. By strengthening legal frameworks, implementing policies, and allocating resources, we can establish a robust foundation for preventing elder abuse and ensuring the protection of older adults.

The book has explored the critical role of support services and therapeutic approaches in assisting elder abuse survivors. Trauma-informed care, counseling, support groups, and access to resources are essential components of healing and recovery for older adults who have experienced mistreatment. These services should be comprehensive, culturally sensitive, and easily accessible to ensure that survivors receive the necessary support they need to rebuild their lives.

Furthermore, the book has shed light on the global perspectives and challenges surrounding elder abuse. By examining cross-cultural perspectives, we understand that elder abuse manifests differently in different cultural contexts. Recognizing cultural norms, values, and practices is crucial in developing effective interventions and strategies that respect diversity and promote collaboration within communities.

Creating a world free from elder abuse requires a collective effort from individuals, communities, organizations, and policymakers. It demands a shift in societal attitudes, the implementation of comprehensive prevention strategies, the provision of accessible support services, and the enactment of robust legal frameworks. By prioritizing the rights, dignity, and well-being of older adults, we can work towards a society that cherishes and protects its elder population.

Let this book serve as a call to action, inspiring individuals to become advocates for older adults, communities to foster inter-generational harmony, organizations to prioritize elder abuse prevention, and policymakers to enact policies that safeguard the rights of older adults. Together, we can create a future where elder abuse is eradicated, older adults are respected, and every individual can age with dignity, security, and the support they deserve.

www.ingramcontent.com/pod-product-compliance
Lightning Source LLC
LaVergne TN
LVHW061551070526
838199LV00077B/6991